A History of the I
Downl

by Robin Pearl

Published by Robin Pearl
Little Downham

Email: robinpearl@hotmail.com

ISBN   978-1-5272-8500-2

First published 2021

Table of Contents

Acknowledgements

Ely Standard for allowing the reproduction of historical newspaper cuttings.

The Cambridgeshire Collection for allowing the reproduction of archive photographs and the use of their newspaper archive.

Cambridgeshire Archives

John Heaps for allowing the use of Cyril Heaps' memoirs.

The history of the Bishop's Palace   Mark Stevens

History of the Few family   Peter Hampson

Sales Posters   Pat Ashton

Emma Martin for proof reading this book and helping to turn it into a correct and readable form of English.

The following people have contributed to this book by posting comments on Facebook or relating memories to me personally both recently and in the past.

Catherine Adams, Debbie Adams-Payne, Emma Ambrose, Clare Andrews, Pat Ashton, Anna Bailey, Amie Barrett, Charlie Beagle, Karl Bedingfield, David Bedingfield, Pauline Bedingfield McCamant, Margaret Belam, Melinda Bidwell, Catherine Booth, Tracy Bradbury, Sarah Brooks, Jean Burkitt, Shaun Butcher, Alan Butcher, Stewart Bye, Donna Callaby, Albert Casbon, Colin Chambers, Karen Champion, Penny Chase, Amy Clifford, Sam Clifton-Noble, Julie Cooper, Julie Cox, Roy Crane, Lou Crane, Jenny Curtis, Kevin Daily, Bridget Dawkis, Ann Deighton, Jean Dowden, Gareth Draper, Fred Duffield, Alice Easy, Andy Emery, Mike England, Gwyneth Evans Miller, Jayne Foulds, Angela Fox, Denise Freear, Charlie Gienke, Stephen Gilbert, Fraser Gilbert, Stephen Glover, David Glover, John Glover, Audrey Glover, Adam Golding, Matt Golding, Lucy Goodfellow, Trudy Goodjohn, Philipa Gott, Hollie Graham, Denise Gudgeon, Peter Hampson, Carol Harley, Dawn Harris, Jean Harrison, Michael Harrison, Judy

Harrison, Vivian Haylock, Graham Hayter-Smith, John Heaps, Cyril Heaps, Bill Heaps, Colin Hills, Frances Hirst, Peter Hobbs, Andrew Hopkirk, Sally Anne Howard, Kath Ingram, Vickie Jameson, Diana Jillian, Tracy Johnson, Cheryl Jordan, Ian Kidd, Gary King-Hall, Tanya Knighton, Lucy Kynaston, Graham Lark, Kathleen Lark, Donna Leonne, Frank (Dempsey) Lythell, Colin Lythell, Jane Mace, Alan Martin, Roger Martin, Helena Martin, Stan Martin, Valerie Mason, Heather Maunders, Margaret Missen, Philip Morton, Diane Munns, Bhavna Narotam, Alan Newark, Mark Nicholas, Lucy Oakes, Julie Ostler, Val Padget, Sue Pamby, Cynthia Parsons, Stuart Pawsey, Chris Pearson, Richard Pearson, Roy Pearson, Penny Pearson, Lillian Petitfor, Elaine Pettengell, Mike Petty, Ann Pixley, Tricia Pope, Jackie Preciuk, Jack Proctor, John Reed, Cheryl Reynolds, Jason Reynolds, Sarah Reynolds Hammersley, Kerry Robbins, Kerry Rutterford, Daniel Saberton, Richard Saberton, Andrew Michael Saunders, Charlotte Scotting, Sharon Sharpe, Steve Shipp, Tina Simpson, Suzanne Smith, Jan Sow, Simon Staines, Louise Micheala Stearman, Mark Stevens, Tony Summersgill, Lorraine Taylor, Susan Thornton, Janet Tomba, Stephen Tuck, Lorraine Warby, Rod Waters, Valerie Watson, Amanda Wesson, Alan White, Karen Wilson, Pauline Woodbridge, Kate Wright, Jane Wright, Gerald Yardy, Colin Yardy, Linda.

Many people have helped in this project in a variety of ways and I have inevitably omitted some names. Any one who feels that their name has been unjustly left out please contact the author and I will be happy to acknowledge your contribution.

Introduction

The project started with a query about the location of an unknown house. I posted an old photo on the Little Downham Facebook page and received an overwhelming response, with people keen to share memories of the village. This seemed to be an excellent opportunity to collect reminiscences of the community as it used to be. Subsequently, I posted a series of pictures of the village as it is now and asked for people's recollections of the past. Responses came flooding in.

It was evident that many people were keen to share their memories and that others wanted to know the history of their own house.

This book has emerged from these responses by current and former residents of Little Downham, supplemented with my own researches at the Cambridgeshire Archives and the Cambridgeshire Collection at the Cambridge Central Library.

This is not an academic work. I have not referenced every fact to its source nor have I included footnotes to preserve readability and general interest. It must also be born in mind that many of the stories here are oral history. This is history as it is remembered, not necessarily as it happened. Individuals remember the same event with different emphases, locations and outcomes and I have encountered many contradictions when writing up a specific event. I have used my best judgement and further research to record history as near as possible to the facts. However, most of the memories gathered through this project are currently undocumented and, unless written down soon, will be lost forever. I consider it more important to get this oral history recorded than to establish precise facts disregarding everything else.

I have attempted to record the changes that have taken place primarily over the last two hundred years, some of it within living memory. These have been elaborated with stories from the preceding generations as remembered by those that heard them and supplemented by items of interest gleaned from old newspapers and other records. This mainly charts the evolution of the parish from a time when there were shops for all the everyday needs and farmyards that opened up onto the Main Street in the middle of the village. People worked on the farms or in local businesses, there was a railway station, a village policeman and everyone knew everyone else. I have concentrated on the fabric of the parish, the buildings and organisations, and I have passed lightly over the lives of the people and stories of individuals. That is for another book.

Today most shopping needs are met by a trip into Ely to one of four supermarkets, national chain outlets, and specialist local shops, or with a quick search online and a delivery from one of the many vans that drive daily around the parish streets. There are, as I write, a general store, hairdressers, takeaway and bridal shop operating on Little Downham Main Street with no shops in Pymoor. There are two pubs still open and quite a few small businesses around the parish. There are still many farms but employing far fewer people than seventy years ago.

I know that some readers will see not only the history that I have recorded but also the history that I have not, the stories and people that they knew but are not mentioned here, the events that they are sure I got wrong and the places that I missed out. As far as I know, this is the first book about the general history of the Parish of Little Downham. It is not a definitive history but a start for other people to correct and build upon.

A BRIEF HISTORY OF THE PARISH

Downham means the village (ham) on the hill (down). The Little prefix is to distinguish it from the nearby Downham Market. The alternative name of Downham-in-the-Isle locates it geographically in the Isle of Ely. The parish, as it exists in 2021, covers an area in excess of 10,000 acres of which about 7,000 are agricultural fen land. There are also about 1,000 acres of washland. The parish has a population of approximately 2,640 and includes the village of Little Downham, the hamlet of Pymoor with the nearby settlement of Oxlode and, a large agricultural area on the fen with a variety of local names.

Roman jewellery was found when the Bedford level was dug at Gold Hill just over the northern border of the parish and there is an Iron Age fort at nearby Wardy Hill, so this area has a long history of habitation. Downham first appears in the historical records in 971 when the Bishop of Winchester gave it to the monks of Ely.

Little Downham gets a brief entry in the Domesday Book, stating that there were 15 villeins, 8 cottars and, 8 serfs. Villeins were peasants who owed service to the lord of the manor but who farmed land of their own and were relatively wealthy. Cottars were peasants with less land than a villein. A serf was the property of the lord of the manor and had no land.

The early history of the parish is heavily influenced by the Bishops of Ely, who were lords of the manor with the Bishop's Palace and associated estate. The prosperity of Downham is reflected in the manorial records that show an increase in landholders and the building of a new windmill in the 13th century. By the middle of the 14th century the manor estate had shrunk and the manor house was falling into dereliction. Subsequent lessees of the estate influenced the lives of parishioners by the enclosure of land and change of agricultural practices.

Enclosure took place under the General Enclosure Act of 1801 by resolution of a meeting of landowners in 1844. The enclosure map shows that the largest award was made to the Church Commissioners and their land was held under lease by William Martin and Rev. J. H. Sparke, who also held land in their own right. William Martin was based at Manor Farm in Main Street and John Henry Sparke bought Gunthorpe Hall, Mattishall in Norfolk. There are many other landowners named on the map, some with large fields, others with small strips of land. Clare College of Cambridge was also awarded a considerable amount of land.

Another big influence on life in the parish was the draining of the fens. The Romans initiated small drainage projects but the main work was carried out by investors led by the Duke of Bedford in the 17th century. This involved the employment of Dutch engineers, the best known of whom was Cornelius Vermuyden, and they dug the Old Bedford River and the New Bedford River (the Hundred Foot River) which form the northwest boundary of the parish. This had a large effect on the locals who made a living from wildfowling and resulted in the legend of the Fen Tigers, groups of locals who tried to sabotage the drainage projects and maintain their historic way of life. Some of the labour used to dig the Bedford Levels were Scottish prisoners of war from the Battle of Dunbar in 1650 and some of their descendants may well remain in the area.

Modern maps show the northwest parish boundary to be the Old Bedford River at the far side of the washes but old census returns include Purl's Bridge in Little Downham, as do some minutes of the Feoffees charity: however Purl's Bridge is now part of Manea. John Speed's map of 1610 show a river named the Fyrthe Dyke where the Bedford Levels now flow so the drainage scheme has altered the parish boundary.

The village of Little Downham sits on an outcrop of high ground that includes large amounts of sand and gravel. Old maps show a gravel pit on Cannon Street, a brickworks at California and an 1850 advert for a farmhouse fronting Main Street with land extending back towards Cannon Street describes it as having an inexhaustible supply of finest sand and gravel.

In current times the agriculture in the parish is mainly arable with a small amount of grazing, however, the Ordnance Survey map of 1900 shows that the higher land was covered with orchards. Many of the local house owners that I talked to in the process of researching this book told me that part of their house had been used for storing apples. Today most of the original orchards are gone with a few individual trees marking where they were. The Community Orchard has been created to reflect this history with old varieties of Cambridgeshire apples.

The parish charity is known as Little Downham Feoffees but the 1674 accounts book refers to the Town Houses and Grounds charity. Feoffment means the transfer of land or property from one owner to another. Wealthy people would give land to charity by this means and the charity trustees were the Feoffees. In 1700 Robert Cawthorn senior was a Feoffee for the Town Houses and Grounds charity and the name has now been simplified to the Feoffees. In 1917 the Feoffees wrote to the Charity Commission saying that the origin of the charity was unknown.

The Feoffees were originally concerned primarily with the running of the parish schools, providing almshouses and other affordable homes for local people, renting out allotments and farmland and, providing grants for people in need. Today they are no longer responsible for schools and there are no almshouses, only affordable housing. The name of the Feoffees school reflects the charity's traditional role. An entry in the 1880 minutes list sixteen tenants in Feoffees properties as follows:

Pond Lane 2, Main Street 6, Townsend 3, Cross Lane 2, Pymoor 3

Additionally, there were eight properties in School Lane. There are references in the Feoffees minute books to a house in Eagles Lane and also a farmhouse in Frith Head Drove. but their exact location is unclear.

In March 1915 consideration was given as to whether Feoffees properties should be insured against air raids.

The Feoffees provide help to local people in need and had contracts to supply coal to the poor of the parish. In December 1912 It was proposed by the Rector and seconded by Mr Smith that a grant of £1 be made to Mrs Frank Moxon, Main Street, towards the purchase of a new wooden leg. Unfortunately, the local paper reports that, in 1914, Mrs Moxon fell over and broke her other leg. In January 1918 It was proposed that the sum of two pounds each be given to procure comforts and food to the following soldiers who are prisoners of war in Germany: James Cornwell, Horace Taylor, George Lea, E Miller. The trustees also had an eye towards improving the life of the parish and in 1892 arrangements were made for a course of lectures on butter and cream cheese making.

Today the Feoffees consists of twelve trustees; six co-opted by the sitting trustees and six appointed by the parish council. In addition, the village rector is entitled to join the trustees and they employ a clerk. The Feoffees currently own two houses in Pymoor, twenty-two in Little Downham and approximately 194 acres of land in the parish. Some of the houses are currently undergoing renovation.

The parish council consists of eleven councillors and currently employ a clerk and a handyman. They own the playing fields in Little Downham and Pymoor and also the Nature reserve (except for the Community Orchard which is held on a 60-year lease from the County Council). They also maintain a website; www.littledownham.net.

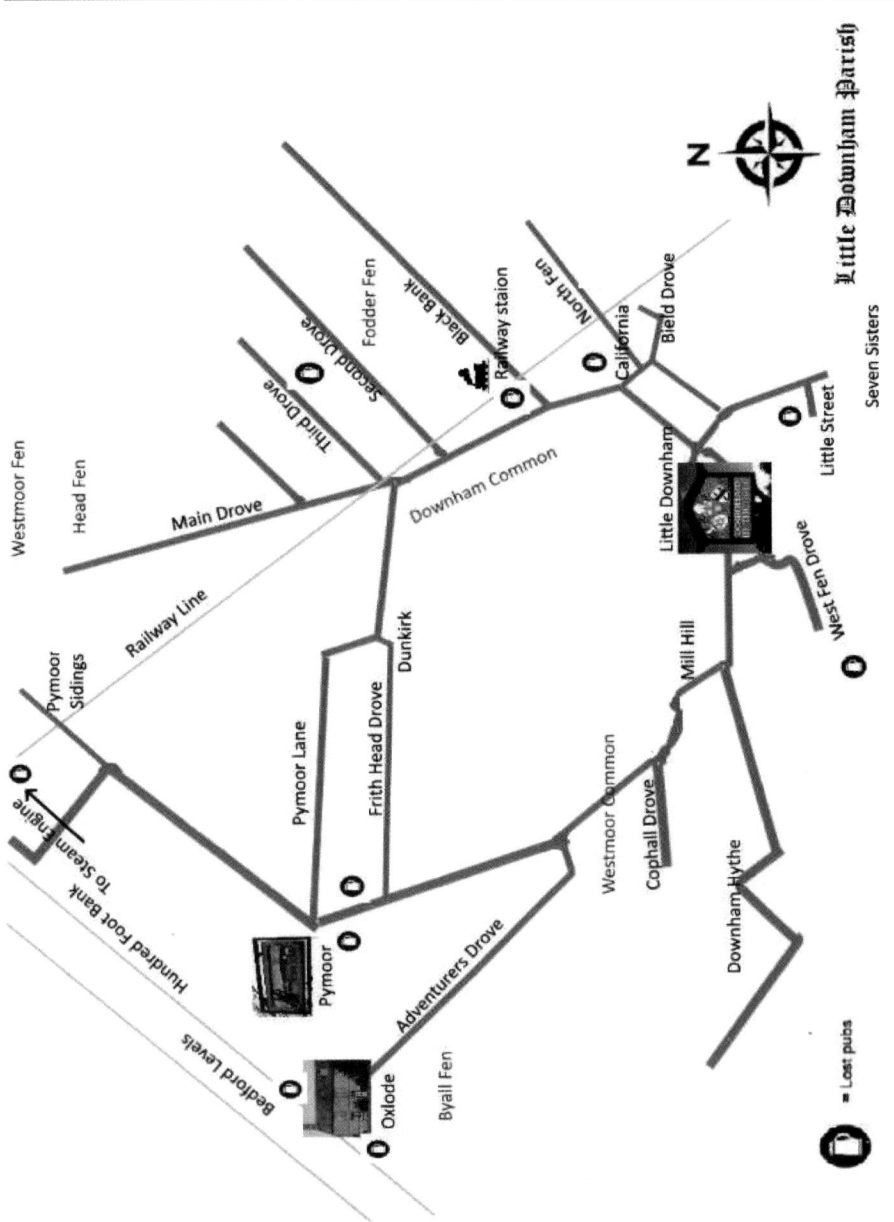

Little Downham Parish

Westmoor Fen
Head Fen
Main Drove
Third Drove
Second Drove
Fodder Fen
Black Bank
Railway staion
North Fen
California
Bield Drove
Downham Common
Little Downham
Little Street
Seven Sisters
West Fen Drove
Railway Line
Pymoor Sidings
To Steam Engine
Hundred Foot Bank
Bedford Levels
Pymoor Lane
Frith Head Drove
Dunkirk
Pymoor
Adventurers Drove
Oxlode
Byall Fen
Westmoor Common
Cophall Drove
Mill Hill
Downham Hythe

= Lost pubs

9

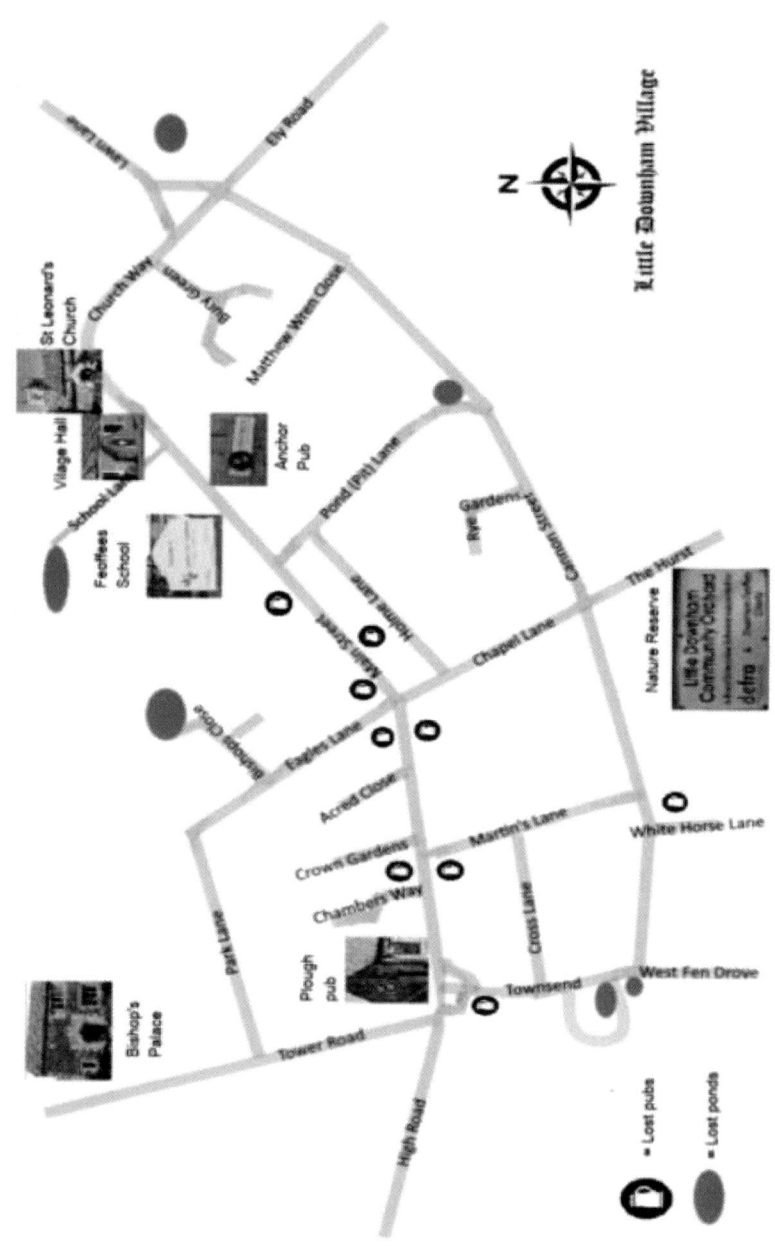

Little Downham Village

N

St Leonard's Church
Village Hall
Feoffees School
School Lane
Church Way
Grimm's Way
Matthew Wren Close
Anchor Pub
Pond (Pit) Lane
Ely Road
Bishops Close
Supply Lane
Eagles Lane
Acred Close
Crown Gardens
Chambers Way
Martin's Lane
Chapel Lane
Carinen Street
Garden
The Hurst
Nature Reserve
Little Downham Community Orchard
defra
White Horse Lane
Cross Lane
West Fen Drove
Townsend
Plough pub
Park Lane
Tower Road
Bishop's Palace
High Road

= Lost pubs
= Lost ponds

LITTLE DOWNHAM VILLAGE

Bishop's Palace

There has been a monastery on this site since at least the 10th century when there would have been monastic buildings, kitchen gardens and fish ponds. First mention of associated parkland is in 1250 when it contained 250 acres. The Bishop of Ely was lord of the manor and the current buildings are the remains of a palace built in the late 15th century by Bishop John Alcock, Bishop of Ely 1486 – 1500. He was also responsible for building the palace in Ely and Jesus College, Cambridge. The stone used came from Barnack at Peterborough and the same style of building can be seen in all three foundations. There was a vacancy in the See during the Elizabethan period and when Bishop Andrewes took over in the reign of James I, he renovated the palace. It fell into disuse during the Civil War after Bishop Matthew

Wren was arrested there in 1642 and the manor was sold off by the Commonwealth. The church regained the estate after 1660 although it was never used as a palace again. When it was demolished much of the stone was used for building in London, although some was used locally and can be found in houses around the village.

Of the remaining buildings, the western one was the refectory with accommodation above and is now used as a shop, currently Equicentric. The middle of the three old buildings is a Georgian farmhouse built on the foundations of the medieval buildings incorporating part of the original gable end. The eastern building is sometimes referred to as the chapel but was probably the gatehouse. It is now private accommodation.

In 1710 the church were granted permission to rent out the land and the remains of the palace became the farmhouse variously known as Park Farm, Tower Farm and Tower Park Farm. As well as the main farm, there is also Low Farm which was halfway between the main farm and Dunkirk. This is not to be confused with Park Farm at Station Road.

As the result of two legal cases Dalton v Girdlestone and Girdlestone v Knight the estate was put up for sale in 1843:

At the Public Sale Room in the Gray's Inn Coffee-house. Holborn, London, on Wednesday, the 14th day of June, 1843, at twelve o'clock noon, in two lots:

An estate, situate at Downham, in the Isle of Ely, in the County of Cambridge, called the Downham Park Estate, containing 694A 1R 21P., or thereabouts, and held under leases for lives from the Bishop of Ely.

The estate was bought by William Smith Simpson who died in 1868. This was when the Stockdale family first became associated with the farm and, on the 1871 census return, Thomas Stockdale from Terrington St John's is farming 408 acres employing 8 labourers and 3 boys. By 1891 William Edward Stockdale had taken over the farm.

William was the son of Samuel Stockdale of Leverington, who ran a peppermint distillery. His relationship to Thomas is not clear.

DEATH OF MR. W. E. STOCKDALE.

Downham Loses a Valued Resident.

AFTER A BRIEF ILNESS.

Residents of Little Downham and the surrounding district heard with profound regret on Friday morning of the death of Mr. William Edward Stockdale, at The Tower, Little Downham. Mr. Stockdale had only been ill a few days, and no fears were entertained for his recovery until Thursday, when his condition became serious, and despite the most careful medical and nursing attention, he passed away in the early hours of Friday morning.

Mr. Stockdale, who had spent more than 40 years of his life in Little Downham, was one of the best-known farmers in the district for miles around. He was also a breeder of the best sense of the word of Shire horses, with which he had obtained many successes at different shows in the Isle, and was one of the principal winners at this year's show at Littleport. His almost sudden demise at the age of 63 came as a great blow, not only to his family, but to his large circle of friends throughout the district.

A son of the late Mr. and Mrs. Samuel Stockdale, of Leverington, near Wisbech, Mr. Stockdale devoted many years of his busy life in the service of the public. Taking part in four elections, he served on the Isle of Ely County Council from March, 1907, to February, 1919, and was a valued member of the Education, Diseases of Animals, Highways and Bridges, Local Government Acts, and Small Holdings Committees. He was also a member of the Ely Rural District Council, on which he first sat on April 29th, 1910, and retained his seat until April 10th, 1919, in which year he retired, as he did from the Little Downham Parish Council, to which he was elected in 1910. Of this body he became Chairman in 1913, and occupied the position with conspicuous success for six years. As well as being a life member of the Feoffees, Mr. Stockdale was a member of many years' standing of the Littleport and Downham Drainage Commissioners, and while he resided in Cambridge-road, Ely, from 1907 to 1926, he was a churchwarden at St. Mary's Parish Church, and in 1917 was elected to the Ely Burial Board, on which he remained until 1927.

Mr. Stockdale, who married a daughter of the late Mr. T. H. Granger, J.P., of Ely, is survived by his wife and one son—Mr. F. H. G. Stockdale, of Cambridge, who has been associated with his father in the business. The other son, Mr. E. L. J. Stockdale, who held the rank of lieutenant in the 10th Lancashire Fusiliers, was killed while serving overseas with that regiment.

William had two sons who both served in the army:

Edward Leslie Johnson Stockdale was baptised at Little Downham in 1893. He was a lieutenant in the 10th Lancashire Fusiliers. Edward was killed in France in 1916 and is commemorated on the war memorial at St Leonard's Churchyard.

Francis Holland Granger Stockdale was baptised at Little Downham in 1895. Francis also joined the army and in 1919 was sent to the Waziristan area of British India where he was promoted to captain. Francis wrote a memoir of his time there entitled "Walking Warily in Waziristan" of which his family published a few copies in the 1980s.

After William's death the farm was tenanted by William Woods Green who later moved to Bury Farm but then Francis Stockdale, by now a major, returned to take it over. Francis had three children, Anne Leslie Stockdale, baptised in Little Downham in 1923, David Lawrence Stockdale, baptised in Cambridge in 1927 and Timothy Edward Stockdale, baptised in Little Downham in 1940.

10-year-old Gerald Yardy used to clean Major Stockdale's boots and shoes for 2s 6d a week and, on Fridays, workers had to stand to attention to receive their wages from major Stockdale.

David later took on the running of the farm. Under the later Stockdales Park Farm become one of the few remaining dairy farms in the area with small fields and pasture land but the dairy industry was unprofitable and the farm fell into disrepair. The family were forced to sell to pay death duties and it was bought by a pension fund which was mainly interested in investing in arable land.

Les Stevens bought the farm in 1980 after running the business for W. B. Chambers on Main street for many years. Les had married Doreen, an evacuee from London who had been living with the Chambers family. When the Stevens bought the farm most of the buildings were derelict, they lived in the Georgian farmhouse whilst restoring the other buildings. The gatehouse was used for keeping cows and the upstairs was an apple store.

Door to the first recorded indoor toilet in England

The internal floors of the barn had been removed and there was a concrete pit in the floor to accommodate a grain silo, although the medieval roof remained and there were medieval decorations on the plaster of the gable wall. After the Stevens had been here for about two years the barn, which was now used as part of a riding centre, was destroyed by fire. The brick structure survived and it was rebuilt with a new roof and stone windows. The barn was used as a restaurant, then an antiques centre, then as offices for Rowley Fine Art and it is now Equicentric, a shop for equestrian equipment. The barn was originally the refectory for the palace with the position of a large oven still visible which was large enough to take a dozen sheep, and a chamber for smoking meat built into the side of the oven. Although the farm is called Tower Farm there is no record of a tower ever being on this site. It is thought that the large oven would require a large chimney, now gone, and that this gave rise to the name.

Above the refectory was accommodation and there is a window in the gable end where there was once a door which accessed the first recorded internal garderobe in England. The brickwork containing the toilet is now gone.

Behind the farm buildings were two tied cottages which Les Stevens sold to a publican from Cambridge for a weekend holiday cottage, they eventually moved there and started an old peoples home in the1980s which is now The Firs Residential Care Home.

Thatched Dovecote

Behind the buildings are extensive gardens which would have once included a kitchen garden for the monastery and beyond those a fish pond which also provided food for the monastery. A medieval wall is built across the top of a well so that water can be drawn from both sides. The field between the palace and Park Lane has a series of low mounds which show the location of old monastic buildings. A thatched dovecote once stood in the middle of this field but was demolished in 1950.

There was a grass landing strip somewhere on the farm in the first war, it was called Tower Farm to avoid confusion with Downham Market. There may also have been a landing strip for spotter planes in the second war as there was a pole on the gable end of the barn with a light on top, said to have been a navigation light for the landing strip.

The signal box which fell into disuse when Black Bank station was closed was bought by Les Stevens for £100 and now sits in the garden in front of the old gatehouse. The farmland is now rented to Mott Farms and consists of about 450 acres.

There has long been a rumour of a secret tunnel between the palace and St. Leonard's Church. An old cowhand who worked on the farm by the name of Vic Juby claimed to the Stevens family that he had been down into the entrance part of the tunnel. There was supposedly a trapdoor just inside the entrance to the gatehouse which required the front door to be bolted so that the trap door could be lifted. There was then a cellar-like chamber which extended out under the door towards the garden. Over the centuries the floor levels have been raised and the trapdoor lost. When the current owner replaced the floor he dug down about three feet to see if he could find anything but there was only rubble backfill to raise the floor level and he didn't investigate any further.

It seems unlikely to me that there would be a tunnel as far as the church but I think that there may have been a priest hole or hiding place. If it did exist there may well still be a chamber underground waiting to be discovered.

Black Bank Drove and Station Road

There are no entries in the 1841 census for this area, and it would seem to have become important with the opening of the railway in 1847. Station Road runs from the end of Lawn Lane to Black Bank. On early maps there are two rights of way running next to each other separated by a ditch, the northern way was Black Bank Drove and to the south of the ditch was The Slipe, which ran from Station Road to where Wood Fen Lodge now stands. Slipe is a dialect word meaning a thin strip of land.

Photo Courtesy Cambridgeshire Collection

By 1851 there were the families of three farmers and a station clerk living at Black Bank and Joseph Crabbe, a turf labourer living at Slipe, North Fen. The Slipe appears listed adjacent to Black Bank in 1861 and over the following fifty years the population of Black Bank and The Slipe remains as a few farmers, the station master, and a coal merchant.

Site of the Railway Tavern, Black Bank

The arrival of the railway also brought the Railway Tavern, which was on the left as you leave the village and just before the railway. The pub first appears in the census in 1861 when John Stevens was the landlord. John later becomes a coal merchant, probably taking delivery of coal from the railway and then delivering it locally. The tavern was taken over by Hezekial Graham a farmer and publican who stays here for over thirty years. He was succeeded by William Jordan, who is there in 1904 when the pub was owned by The William Cutlack Brewery of Littleport.

A GRAND OLD BEERHOUSE.

Black Bank Tavern Closed

GREAT FEATS OF FORMER DAYS.

The doors of the Railway Tavern at Black Bank Station were closed to the public and the last bottle of sparkling ale was sold on Saturday evening. This grand old beerhouse, the taproom constructed of wood and private part bricks, has served a very useful purpose for something like a hundred years, and thousands of traders, farmers, teamsmen and travellers using the railway station, have within its walls been supplied with the needs of bodily sustenance. In days of yore farmers and labourers attended nightly for news, light refreshments and amusements. Smoking concerts and skittles, darts and domino competitions were regularly held.

Many great individual feats have been recorded in the bar. On one occasion, it is said, before the introduction of the reaper and self binder, a villager well used to a scythe, mowed (his wife gathering and tying it after him) more than two acres of corn in 12 hours

FOR 8s. 6d. PER ACRE.

Another vilager in seven hours, threw 16 holes of clay, while a third in an hour's less time, sowed 30 bags of manure on six acres of potato land. The late Kon Moxon, the village 100 yards sprinter, once ran a mile, climbed up the sign post and jumped over both railway gates for a pint of beer, and the remarkable feat of a gentleman who stood on his head in the taproom and drank two pints of beer is still fresh in the memory of those of riper years.

The Railway Tavern was closed in 1933 and there is a small hut remaining on the site which contains an old copper for heating water and may have been the wash house for the pub.

Opposite the Railway Tavern is Slipe Cottage, which still stands, shown with some associated outbuildings on old maps and there is a footbridge across the ditch between the two rights of way, presumably allowing the inhabitants of the cottage easy access to the pub and railway station.

In 1901 the surveyor reported to Ely District Council on the state of Black Bank Drove stating that there was too much heavy traffic to Black Bank Station. The chairman said that as there was a prospect of the road being taken over by the County Council he suggested that it be widened to its full width. The surveyor was instructed to have the road widened to 12ft.

The Slipe was incorporated into the fields and there is no longer any trace of it.

1934

DOWNHAM NONAGENARIAN.

Interesting Memories of Bygone Days.

Hearty congratulations from a host of his relatives and friends were bestowed on Mr. John Butcher, of Slipe Farm, Black Bank, who, on Monday, celebrated quietly his 92nd birthday. Hale and hearty, Mr. Butcher, although retiring from business as a farmer, in favour of his grandsons, a few years ago, still takes a keen interest in the work on the farm. Residing with his grand-daughter, Miss Edith Hall, he is very jovial, exceedingly happy and always ready to crack a joke. In favourable weather he can frequently be seen driving himself to and from the village in a small low trap, hauled by a pretty little Shetland pony, which is well over the age of 20. Possessing an excellent memory, he is able to relate many interesting and amusing events of his boy-

hood days. Commencing work at the age of nine, his wages were 2s. per week and he had to lose wet time. His sister, who worked with him two years older, received 2s. 6d. The working hours were 6 a.m. to 6 p.m. in summer and a trifle less in winter. At that time the farmers were doing well, wheat was making £5 per quarter and other commodities were also selling well. Men's wages were only 8s. per week for ordinary labourers, but horsekeepers and shepherds received a 1s. more. Some sixty years ago, said Mr. Butcher, hundreds of acres of claying was annually done on the big farms in winter months. He had thrown thousands of holes in his time for 4½d per hole. Extraordinary crops of corn always followed a good coat of clay, and as many as 15 coombs of wheat per acre have afterwards been grown. On one occasion Mr. Butcher mowed forty coombs of wheat in two days and a friend of his, who recently passed away, at the age of 90, once mowed two acres, a good crop, in one day on two pints of four ale for 8s. per acre. Mr. Butcher has still living, a sister at Wisbech, one brother in the village, and another brother at Littleport. The combined ages of the sister and three brothers total, in the aggregate, approximately 325 years.

In February 1953 the War Department wrote to the Feoffees asking if they had any claim arising out of the defence works at Slipe Drove when the Slipe was widened, spoil deposited on the adjoining drove, and two wooden bridges removed. The Feoffees made no claim.

Station Road runs from California to Black Bank Drove. There is one farm on this stretch of road, Park Farm, which marks the eastern edge of the Bishop's Palace deer park. Park Farm has a claim to fame with Wilfred the Bull who was well known locally through appearances at fetes and who, along with his owner Ron Gillett, appeared on the

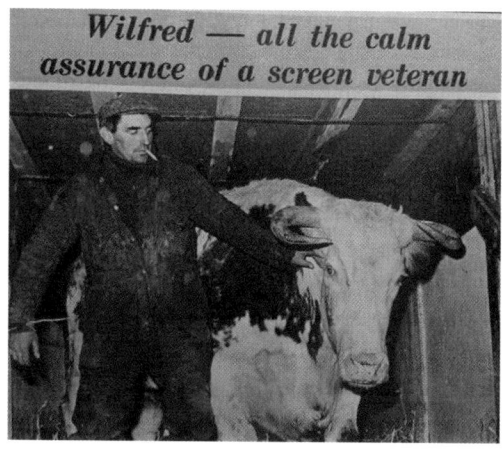

Wilfred — all the calm assurance of a screen veteran

children's television programme, Blue Peter.

This 31-year-old Dodge lorry, claimed by its owner, Mr. Ron Gillett, of Park Farm, Little Downham, to be the oldest working lorry in the area, is pictured on its farewell trip to Ely Beet Sugar factory on Thursday.

The reliable five ton lorry, which in 31 sugar beet campaigns has transported over £½ million worth of beet for the Gillett's and their neighbours, is one of the victims of a recent transport ruling.

Lorries are now not allowed to carry loads exceeding their body weight, so the Dodge is bowing out.

It is being replaced by a brand new 11 ton Bedford articulator.

However, the Dodge's working days are not completely over for Mr. Gillett plans to use the lorry's trailer behind a tractor.

At the junction with Station Road and Black Bank is a modern house which is part of Park Farm

Station Road only appears in the census returns in 1891 and seems to be included under the name Black Bank in other years.

Black Bank Railway Station

The Great Eastern Railway opened the Ely-Peterborough line in 1847 and Little Downham station was opened on 14th Jan 1847. In 1853 the name was changed to Black Bank to avoid confusion with Downham station (now Downham Market). As well as a regular service there were special excursions to places such as Wisbech, Great Yarmouth, Nottingham Goose fair, Peterborough fair and Hunstanton. The coming of the railway brought about the revival of the ancient market at March and a

LITTLE DOWNHAM.

SUNDAY EXCURSION.—Twenty parishioners boarded at Black Bank the special half-day excursion train to London on Sunday.

boom in the number of coaches between Wisbech and March to catch the trains.

The station occasionally made the news, usually because of an accident. In 1854 two goods trains ran into each other head-on at the station in the fog. The engines were destroyed but the drivers were able to jump clear before the contact. In July 1908 Harold Lofts, age

18, started work at the station as a porter. The next day he was knocked down by a train and killed.

In 1929 the LNER decided to introduce a best kept stations award. Black Bank was inspected in July, porter W. E. Crane was highly complimented on the splendid condition of the lamps and signalman Goodchild was congratulated on a beautifully clean signal box. Also in 1929 proposals were made for a new reception line on the up side between Black Bank and Chettisham stations. This meant that slow goods and coal trains could be run into the reception line at Black Bank to allow passenger and express goods trains to pass along the main line.

In the 1950s the station was suffering from subsidence and needed rebuilding, the top floor of the station master's house had already been demolished. There were nine trains a day stopping at Black Bank but a passenger survey carried out in February 1962 found that passenger

numbers joining and alighting from the trains were seven on weekdays and five on Sundays. The annual saving to the railway if the station were to close would be £240 and a spokesman said that traffic now using the station will be accommodated by buses. The Isle of Ely County Council decided not to raise any objections to the withdrawal of passenger and parcel services although there was one written objection to the closure from a member of the public. The passenger services ended on 17th June 1963.

The retirement of Mr Herbert Thomas Aspland, signalman at Black Bank station, in 1932 was reported in the local paper and illustrates the developments that took place over his time with the railway, which extended over a period of nearly half a century. He started as a boy porter at Black Bank on 5th August 1886 and then went to Chettisham and Ely. In 1889 he was promoted to signalman at Coldham, then to Stonea and Black Bank, where he served under five different station masters. In his time at the station loads of goods and coal trains increased from 35 to 80 trucks and empty truck trains from 50 to 100 wagons. Block telegraph working was transformed and the telephone replaced the single needle instruments. Hours of labour have reduced from 12 to 8, wages have been increased, in some cases by more than 100 percent, and the annual holiday extended from three to six days. On his retirement Mr Aspland was presented with a Westminster chimes clock.

Goods facilities were withdrawn in April 1965 amid protests from coal and potato merchants. Ely was designated as the alternative depot for on and off loading of the ware and seed potatoes, coal and raw sugar beet which had formed the principal freight traffic. The signal box, thought to have been built in the mid 19th century, was taken out of use in 1988.

California, Brick Kiln Lane and North Fen

The first question here is how did California come to be so called? There are three possible explanations:

1/ According to a book called 'The Place Names of Cambridgeshire and the Isle of Ely' by P. H. Reaney, places away from the centre of a village were given names of places far away as an ironic name. He gives examples of Scotland, Yorkshire and Dunkirk.

2/ When the railways were built the navvies set up encampments nearby and gave them exotic names. The name first appears in the mid-1800s when the railway was being built.

3/ The explanation for California Cliffs in Cromer is that the railways brought so much trade for businesses that they were like a goldmine and so the area was called California after the gold rush. It may be that the navvies brought a lot of trade to the local pub there (the Brickmakers Arms) and local traders did a lot of business there.

RAT-CATCHER APPOINTED

ELY URBAN COUNCIL on Monday, on the recommendation of Couns. J. W. Clarke and W. M. Brown, Chairman and Vice-Chairman respectively of the Public Health and Water Committee, appointed Mr. C. Yardy, aged 35, of 1, California, Little Downham, as rat-catcher. With two other candidates from Littleport and Girton, Mr. Yardy was interviewed by Couns. Clarke and Brown. There was a fourth applicant for the post, a 73-year-old man from Saffron Walden.

The name California derives from a 16th century novel by a Spanish author, Garcia Ordonez de Montalvo. The novel described an island, very close to the Garden of Eden, full of gold, which was ruled by strong and beautiful black women. The California gold rush took place between 1848 -1855 and it starts to come into use as a place name around East Anglia in the 1840s

The first reference to the name at Little Downham is in November 1856 when John Lucas, a fish dealer, is charged with stealing a blue pilot coat, a silver watch, a gold ring and a pair of gloves from the person of Ephraim Ruth, a pensioner, whilst in a state of drunkenness, at the California beer shop, Downham. The first reference in the parish registers to someone being from California is the burial of Robert Pate in 1857.

Black Bank Station opened in January 1847 which is just before the gold rush brought the name to prominence but does not necessarily preclude the navvies theory.

The 1885 Ordnance Survey map shows California as an area consisting of the Brickmakers Arms (now Bield House) and four semi-detached houses. Opposite these was the brickworks. The only other buildings are at Brick Kiln Farm, opposite North Fen. In 1887 four cottages with gardens at California were advertised for sale.

There is no reference to California or any residences here in the 1841 census, Richard Fisher, a shepherd, and family lived at Bield Drove, Joseph Lofts, a turf merchant, and family lived at North Fen and Fails Taylor and family were at Brick Kiln Farm. Ten years later five families of farm labourers were living at Brick Lane.

In 1857 there was a sale of leaseholds on property owned by Mr Tingey and Mr Crawley. This included a newly built substantial brick and slate beer house at Brick Kiln Lane, in Downham, called the Brickmakers Arms. Comprising three rooms below, four chambers, roomy cellar and convenient granary attached. It is currently let to William Ward at £13 per annum.

> Entering his cottage at the North Fen Railway Crossing, on Monday, Mr. W. Holland, a platelayer at Black Bank, was amazed to find a snake on the dinner table snugly curled three times round the sugar basin apparently sleeping with its head under the edge of the tea tray. After calling Mr. Frank Glover, a neighbour, Mr. Holland seized a suitable weapon and immediately ended the life of the intruder. Mr. Holland stated afterwards it was a mystery as to how this reptile, measuring over three feet in length, obtained access to the house as all doors and windows had been closed several hours previously.

The Brickmakers Arms is thought to have closed in the early 1950s and was bought by Sid Martin who farmed at Bield Drove.

North Fen leads to North Fen Farm, a cottage called Millcroft, the railway crossing and a cottage near the parish boundary. In 1941 there was only one resident in North Fen, Joseph Lofts, a turfman. The population expanded over the years to include farmer William Moxon and family, whose holding gradually expanded from 30 to 80 acres, and a railway worker in a cottage by the crossing.

In 1939 there are 5 households living in North Fen including James and Ada Foreman, James was a railway worker and Ada the crossing keeper. Within living memory, there was a farm called Millhurst near the railway line owned by Frank and Mildred Glover, which they originally shared with the Long family but the Glovers eventually took on the whole farm. The Frank family lived in a house on the other side of the railway that has now gone and there was a small house opposite North Fen Farm also now disappeared. The last tenants of the railway house were the Beresfords, again this house has gone.

There is a cottage in California called Besoughan. The current owner tells me that it was built on the foundations of outbuildings from the former pub and has since been expanded. The original owner was a newspaper reporter, Mr Anderton, who named it after the village in Belgium where he met his wife when reporting on the first war. The village was destroyed in the war.

Cannon Street

There is a story that the street is named after an incident when a cannon was set up in the road and fired at Ely Cathedral, but I think that this is only a story. The 1900 Ordnance Survey map shows only three houses between Ely Road and where Oak Farm Drive is now, a pair of cottages where numbers 19 and 21 now stand and a cottage in the location of Rye Gardens. Numbers 19 and 21 were two of several properties that were owned by the Thompson family. There was a gravel pit on the eastern corner of Chapel Lane and a pond on the green at Pond Lane. By 1925 the gravel pit was gone, Cathedral view had appeared, and there was a house possibly now the one numbered 44 or close to that site.

The houses on Cannon Street have been renumbered as new properties have been built and so the numbers referred to in old documents do not correspond to today's houses.

Some of the older and more notable buildings are as follows:

Saberton Blacksmiths

Photo Courtesy Philip Laver

Photo Courtesy Philip Laver

The space between numbers 5 and 7 which, as I write, is being used as the access to a new estate under development, was the site of Peter Saberton's blacksmith workshop. Peter was the son of Frank Saberton who started as a Blacksmith with the Bysouth wheelwright family and then took over his father's business in Main Street opposite the village hall. He then moved the business to this site in Cannon Street, where he lived. This family can be traced back to the Saberton family of Blacksmiths at the Club Inn on Main Street.

Cathedral View

A large house stood here that was the home of the Saberton family on the western corner of the junction with Pond Lane.

It was put up for auction by Mrs A. A. Fuller in 1944 whilst it was being rented to Richard Saberton at £20 a year and it was bought by the Saberton family for £800. It was described as a dwelling house and orchard on an area of about 3 roods and 23 poles. The orchard was fully planted with apple and plum trees.

A large black shed stood next to the house and that was where the Sabertons started their potato business and became the home of A. L. Saberton potato merchant. This has now moved to Fitzballe house on Main Street. These buildings have now gone and have been replaced by a row of new houses.

Petrol station at Downham

Ely R.D.C. Housing Committee have recommended approval for the erection of a motor service and repair shop, and petrol station at the corner of Chapel-lane and Cannon-street, Little Downham.

The Committee recommended approval of the application by Mr. J W H Lock of 45 Main-street, Little Downham despite adverse planning observations by the council's engineer and surveyor, Mr. R J Williams.

Mr. Williams thought that approach roads would be inadequate for the increased traffic. The proposal would be visible for a considerable distance and the area should be reserved for residential development only.

The committee, however, thought it would be a good idea to get traffic off the main road.

This petrol station did not get built

39 Cannon Street (Pingle House)

The Hull family built Pingle House around the turn of the 19th century and lived in it until about 1970. The last of the family living in the house was Annie who taught piano in the front

Horace Hull used to live in Pingle House. He had huge orchards at the back. As kids he would have us picking gooseberries, apples, blackcurrents, pears and, later in the year, walnuts.

room and was an assistant teacher in the village school. The Sudells bought the house 1971-2 and did a major conversion before it was bought in 1975 by Philip and Diane Laver.

The Hull family at Pingle House
Photo Courtesy Philip Laver/Jean Harrison

40 Cannon Street (Fir Tree House)

Newsagent for over 40 years

Paying their last respects to a well-known Little Downham resident, a large congregation assembled at the Baptist Chapel, on Friday for the funeral of Mr. Herbert William Hull, who died at his home, Fir Tree House, 10 Cannon-street, on the previous Tuesday.

Mr. Hull, who was 70 years of age, had been in failing health for about 12 months. Until his recent retirement he was news-agent for the village for over 40 years.

He served in the Cambridge-shire Regiment during the first World War, spending three years in the trenches. He was a regular worshipper at the Baptist Chapel, extremely fond of gard-ening, and found much enjoy-ment in all sport, particularly shooting and fishing.

This was the home of Herbert Hull who ran a newsagents business from here. Herbert was the son of Robert Hull, landlord of the Railway Tavern.

No. 14, CANNON ST., LITTLE DOWNHAM

(3 miles from Ely)

PARTICULARS OF A VALUABLE

FREEHOLD RESIDENCE

Known as "RYE CLOSE"

Together with an INTENSELY CULTIVATED

MIXED ORCHARD

and

PACKING SHED, YARD, POULTRY HOUSE AND PIGGERY

Situate in Cannon Street at the junction of Chapel Lane, with frontages thereto of 362 Ft. 6 ins. and 166 Ft. respectively, being O.S. No. pt. 1375 and containing an

AREA of 1 a. 3 r. 3 p. IN ALL

as occupied by Mr. G. L. Hull who will give

VACANT POSSESSION

on completion of the purchase.

THE RESIDENCE has a due South aspect with extensive views and is exceptionally well built in modern design (white bricks and slated roof). It is detached with double front and has a gravelled Front Garden enclosed by privet hedge. The principal accommodation is of a uniform size of 13 ft. x 13 ft. and the decorative condition (mostly paper) is as new throughout.

On the Ground Floor:

CENTRAL HALL with boarded floor and staircase cupboard; LOUNGE (front) with similar floor and new tiled fireplace in mahogany surround; DINING ROOM (front) with boarded floor and tiled fireplace; MORNING ROOM/KITCHEN with boarded floor and 'Broadcast' cook-an-heat stove; SPACIOUS PANTRY with shelving; CONSERVATORY, 29'8" x 6'6", communicating LODGE (Lean-to) and WASH HOUSE (built-in) with concrete floor, copper and open hearth. Closet with 'Elsan' unit.

On the First Floor:

4 BEDROOMS (one with fireplace and one with 2 windows) all opening on to spacious CENTRAL LANDING.

Electricity Installation with 5 heating plugs and 3 bed switches. E.R.D.C. Water.

THE BUILDINGS comprise a brick and timber built PACKING SHED, 18'6" x 8'9", with concrete floor and c.i. roof; STORE PLACE and a Yard with vehicle access from Cannon Street. There is also a timber and iron roofed DOUBLE PIGGERY fronting a second vehicle access from Cannon Street and a similar built POULTRY HOUSE, 26' x 13'.

THE ORCHARD consists of apple, plum and pear trees of popular varieties and about two-thirds is underplanted with 'Laxton's Perfection' Red Currant and 'Careless' Gooseberry Bushes. The Trees and Bushes have been well managed, with annual replacements as required, and are in full bearing. The Orchard is also highly suitable for residential development.

General and Water Rates £7 18s. 0d. (Rateable Value £12.) Tithe Redemption Annuity 9s. 6d.

VIEW:—By appointment with Mr. G. L. Hull.

FOR SALE BY AUCTION BY

GEORGE COMINS & SON

THE WHITE HART HOTEL, ELY

Thursday, 3rd April, 1952. At 4 p.m.

(Subject to Conditions of Sale to be then produced).

Vendor's Solicitors:
MESSRS. HALL, ENNION & YOUNG
ELY. (Tel. 50). And at York House, LITTLEPORT (Tel. 453) and Haddenham.

AUCTIONEERS' HEAD OFFICES: ELY. (Tel. 65). Branch Office: 30, Churchgate Street, SOHAM (Tel. 264). And at Ely Cattle Market and Burwell.

Oak Farm

Oak Farm Drive is built on the site of Oak Farm. In 1945 the farm was run by Henry Mann, born in Soham and his wife Annie. Henry died in 1937 and when Annie died in 1945 she bequeathed the farm to her daughter Ethel, who married Sidney Murfitt in the same year. A story by Roger Martin that once appeared in the parish magazine says that "A turf fire burned for over 80 years never to be let out in Oak Farm House, Cannon Street, burning both in the winter and summer months." The estate now on this site was developed in 2007.

43 Cannon Street

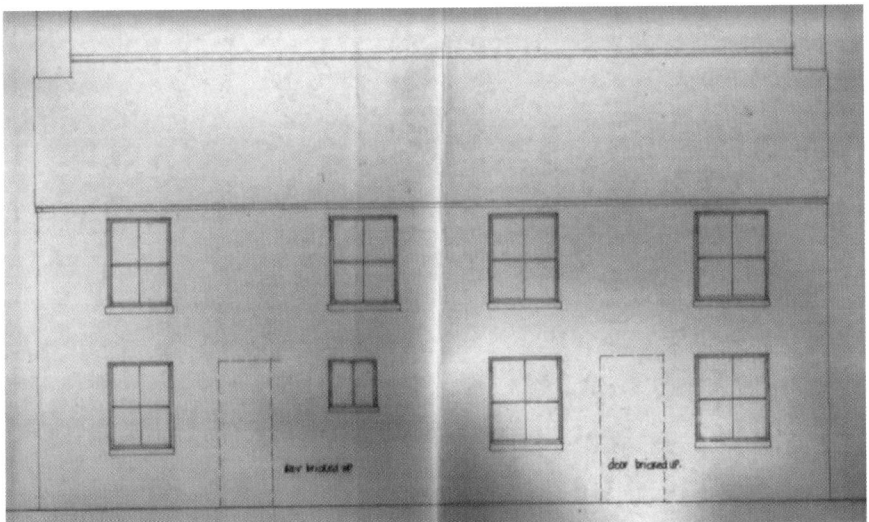

Built in the early 1900s the house here replaced an earlier structure, possibly farm buildings. It was originally two cottages, 43 and 45 later converted to a single house. Like a number on that side of the street, there is a well in the back garden.

51 Cannon Street

This was the home of Gerald and Marjorie Hull, Marjorie was a schoolteacher. Their son Richard lived here after them.

70 Cannon Street

On the 1900 Ordnance Survey map this house is shown as divided into 2 properties and was the home of the Gilbert family. Local gravedigger Reg Gilbert lived in one side and his son the other. The houses opposite number 70 are built on what was once a large square field called Church Gardens. The lease for this land contained clauses prohibiting the drinking of alcohol and building of toilets and it is now farmed by the Gilbert family.

74 and 76 Cannon Street

These two cottages are built on land shown as undeveloped in 1900. The plaque on the front shows that they were built in 1914 for J. H. S. and this probably indicates that they were built as farm workers cottages for John Henry Stevens of Manor Farm on Main Street.

78 and 80 Cannon Street

The two attached cottages here were built in about 1890. Number 80 is home to the Lely family, one of whom helped to build them, and the fourth generation of Lelys to live here has recently been born.

84 (Rose Cottage) to 86 (Honeysuckle Cottage) Cannon Street

I used to live there when it was two houses. We rented the left hand side to a Mrs Morgan and we lived in the other two thirds. I remember the inglenook well, glad it's still there.

These used to be owned by the Diocese of Ely as two houses with the smaller one on the left. There are large inglenook fireplaces in both 84A and 86.

Orchard Cottage and 55 Cannon Street

Here was the home of the Hopkin family (possibly who gave their name to Hopkins Hill) and the names Hopkin and Hopkins seem to be interchangeable in early documents. The Cottage is built on land that is shown on the 1844 enclosure map as belonging to Philip Hopkins.

William Joseph Hopkin and Kate (nee Lewis) were living here in 1911 with two children, William Lewis and Agnes Phyllis, with Arthur John yet to

> Arthur died in 1997, he was a great bloke. He married Joan Thorpe from Pymoor and they lived in Sutton.

be born some time later in 1921. William was a farmer and market gardener and was also described as an orchardist.

Ernest Biddle Chambers lived in part of Orchard Cottage until his death in 1925.

Next to Orchard Cottage, on the site of 55 and 55A stood Pear Tree Farm, another house occupied by the Hopkin Family again on land once owned by Philip Hopkins. In 1911 another William Hopkin, the father of William Joseph, was living here with his second wife Susan (nee Smith) and several children. One of these children, Len, later lived here with his wife Phyllis. Len was a dairy farmer who retired in 1955 and Ernest Chambers bought the farm. Len emigrated with his son Philip to Australia. George Yardy worked for the Chambers and lived in a cottage at the farm. Ron Chambers lived in orchard cottage in the 1950s and 60s.

William Hopkin senior was the son of Philip and Eleanor Hopkin, presumably the Philip who owned the land in 1844. The Hopkin name can be traced back to the first entry in the Little Downham parish registers for the baptism of Mary Hopkin in 1660. Eleanor was born Eleanor (or Ellen) Denston, another old Little Downham family who first appear with Florence Denston married in 1637.

The buildings on this site change considerably between the 1884 and 1900 Ordnance Survey map which suggest that these cottages were built on the site of older buildings. They were built in 1887 and named for Queen Victoria's golden jubilee.

Chapel Lane

There is no mystery about the name of the street as it is the home of the Baptist chapel, built in 1788 with some rebuilding in1858. However, this seems to be one of several examples of a road having an official name and a local name. Old maps always call this Chapel Lane but the 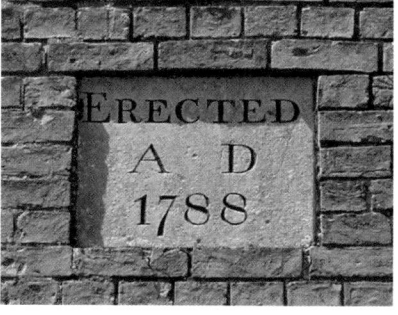 census returns call it Chapel Lane in 1841 but then variously Loft's Lane and Meeting Lane before reverting to Chapel Lane in 1891. Meeting Lane probably alludes to the chapel being called a meeting house. Over the period that the census covers there is only one household in this street although it is a different family at each return and there are no Lofts living here.

Chapel Lane links the Hurst to Eagles Lane and so forms part of the original route between Ely and the Bishop's Palace. As late as 1925 the Ordnance Survey map shows no houses beyond the chapel.

Church Way and Bury Green

There are no houses with Church Way as an address. It is bordered by Bury Green and the village green. There was a large pond in the south-east corner of the green

We live in Bury Green. On our chimney in the loft it has 1972 inscribed on it.

and this area is marked on a map of 1871 as Horse Pond Hill.

Bury Green is a 1970s development that fronts onto Church Way opposite Lawn Lane. Prior to development, it was a farmyard belonging to George Green who lived in Bury House on Main Street,

The pond on the village green, next to my grandfather, Lewis Hull's land, was filled in in the 1960s I believe. I remember skating on there in the 50s.

opposite the village hall, which was then the village school. When corn stacks were being thrashed in the winter some of the schoolboys would go over to the farm to catch mice. George also farmed land in Bield Drove and North Fen. There were a pair of detached houses on the site that were, at one time, occupied by members of the Hull family.

Cowbridge Hall Road and Bield Drove

As everyone in Little Downham knows, this is really called Cabbage Hole Road. It is called Cabbage Hole Drove on the early Ordnance Survey maps, although the earliest map on which it is named, the 1844 enclosure map, labels it as Cow Bridge Road. The census returns all call it Cabbage Hole.

> I know that one of the Saberton families lived along Cabbage Hole, there were two sons, Roger (can't remember the other) and a sister, Janet.

Early maps show only a single house where there are now a pair of cottages that replaced it in 1913. This was presumably the home of Thomas and Elizabeth Cornwell who were long term residents between 1851 and 1901. The only other resident in this period was John Brown, a journeyman blacksmith, who appeared here in 1871, with another house being uninhabited. On the 1939 register George and Maria Lythell were the only family living here.

Bield Drove leads from the end of Cowbridge Hall Road and turns northwards with Coffue Drove continuing eastwards. These Three roads form the northern boundary of a clearly defined set of ancient fields called Hither Bield, owned by a variety of

The original farmhouse at Bield Farm
Photo Courtesy Alan Martin

local landholders, and Further Bield owned by the Bishop of Ely and the Rev John Henry Sparke.

Bield Farm sits in the corner of Bield and Coffue Droves. Since 1841 a number of families have lived here. In 1861 John and Rachel Gibson farmed here with 92 acres employing 2 men and three boys. The farm had expanded when John and Rachel Flanders took over to 150 acres employing 12 men, 1 boy and 3 women. John's son Frederick took on the farm and by 1939 Herbert Martin was here and the Martin family remain here, having briefly moved to Bield House in California, farming cattle.

There was one other dwelling in Bield Drove at the railway crossing and was the home to various employees of the Great Eastern Railway Company, which suggests that they were probably the owners and the house was tied to the job. William Jefferson, a railway platelayer lived here for over twenty years.

As I write in September 2020 Bield Drove has just been surfaced, turning it from a dirt drove into a surfaced road as far as Bield Farm.

> **JUNE 15, 1951**
>
> **BEILD DROVE REPAIRS**
>
> It was reported that Beild Drove was in a very poor state of repair, and it was desirable that repairs should be carried out before the advent of winter. The Council decided that Coun. Darby should approach the Divisional Surveyor at Ely with a view to having the work done, and that if necessary, formal application be made to the City Surveyor.

Alan martin, who now lives at Bield Farm, recalls the changes in the landscape:

The land has shrunk a lot, my father said that in the 1950s you could see a man the other side of the railway from the waist up. Now you can't even see the top of his head. In the field by the side of Bield Drove we always used to hit bog oaks when ploughing but we are getting to the last of them now. A lot of the bog oaks lay east-west as they were blown over by the wind from the west.

Cross Lane

Cross lane runs between Martin's Lane and Townsend, which may be the origin of the name as it crosses between the two, or it may be related to the Cross family which has appeared in the parish registers over the years, starting with George, who was baptised as George Crose in 1669 and married as George Cross in 1698.

No historic buildings remain in Cross lane and there are only a group of three houses where numbers 11, 11A and 11B now stand marked on the 1925 Ordnance Survey map. These were at one time owned by the Feoffees who put two of them up for sale in 1872, described as two brick built cottages in the occupation of John Lofts and another, reserve price £50. In 1915 the Feoffees obtained estimates for repairing the roof of their remaining house with reeds and straw and with corrugated iron. Later the Feoffees again had two cottages in Cross Lane, numbers 7 and 7A, which they decided to sell in 1953 as they were too expensive to maintain. This may not have happened as the minutes for 1965 decided that the two houses in Cross Lane should be condemned and not re-let and two years later it was again decided to sell them.

Towards the northern corner with Townsend was the back of a group of houses fronting onto Main Street known as The Barracks although there were no buildings on Cross Lane.

The census returns show a period of decline and regeneration here as there were ten agricultural labourers living in Cross Lane in 1841 but this had dwindled to a single household, John Simpson, a farmer, by 1871. This rose again to three in 1891, presumably the three houses marked on the map and back up to eleven by 1939.

Eagles Lane

The main road from Ely to Little Downham was originally the Hurst, which is now just a track. This is a direct route from Ely Cathedral to the Bishop's Palace and Eagles Lane is part of this route.

Eagles Lane was nothing more than a drove with thatched cottages at the top and an infants school on the site now occupied by the allotments. It was known locally as Little School Lane, although it is also referred to as Crawley's Lane on some census returns, presumably named after Etches Crawley who was landlord of the Fox and Hounds pub on the corner with Main Street. There is also a record of it being called Fox and Hounds Lane. There was historically an Eagle family in the village with James Eagle being an overseer for the poor in 1692 and they probably gave their name to this road. The 1844 enclosure map shows the land on the west side of the lane was owned by John Simpson and as late as the 1925 Ordnance Survey map there are no buildings beyond the old infants' school. In 1909 there was a complaint to the council about the state of the lane leading to the infants' school. It stated that the children had to play in the Main Road and asked the council to remedy the situation.

In the 1911 census only two households are in Eagles Lane: Alfred Fuller, an entomologist and aquarist, who lived with Sarah Ann Fuller, his housekeeper and Samuel and Sarah Ann Fincham with four children. Samuel was a carpenter.

On the 1901 census William Yardy, a brickmaker from March, with his wife, Ann, and their five children are the only residents. Earlier census returns show three households with families coming and going. The one long term resident was William Fuller, a groom from Chippenham and his wife, Frances, from Burwell. They are here from 1861 to 1891.

A thatched cottage stood behind the Fox and Hounds which was originally the gatehouse to the Bishop's Palace estate. It was owned by the Missen Family who demolished it in the late 1900s when it was replaced by a modern bungalow. Eagles Lane led to Smith's Field, now Bishop's Close.

> *I remember Neil Gooden having the first colour TV anybody had seen. We all used to crowd round the window in their house in Eagles Lane and watch through the window.*

The administration of the properties of Grace Green of Bury House dated 1959 include the following:

All that cottage or tenement formerly divided into two tenements situate in Eagles Lane Downham aforesaid and known as Number 1 Eagles Lane which said property was conveyed to the intestate (Grace Green) by a conveyance dated the Thirtieth day of March One Thousand nine hundred and forty three and made between Ethel Rayner and Edith Eliza Green of the one part and the intestate of the other part.

The building described here no longer exists.

Old Infants' School

Where the allotments are now sited on Eagles Lane stood the old infants school, erected in 1855 by public subscription. It took pupils aged between 5 and 7 years.

The teachers at the school in the 1940s were Miss Knight and Miss Woolnough. Miss Knight was described as 'old school' and misbehaviour was met with a rap across the knuckles.

The children had to walk up to the big school building, now the village hall, for their lunch.

> *I remember the infant school, Miss Knight sat at a high desk, she wore long bloomers and kept her hanky tucked up the leg, we all giggled about that. The toilets were outside around the back. It was a sweet little school which held many happy memories.*

Photo Courtesy David Bysouth

There was a cottage for the school head which was rebuilt in 1871 and again in 1919 at a cost of £530. In 1876 Miss Talls announced her forthcoming marriage but asked to be kept on as Mistress saying it would not affect her duties; the Feoffees agreed.

The school inspection of 1878 resulted in the following report:

This is a nice school room but infants are very ill taught. Their writing is as bad as possible, their reading is indifferent.

Just one large room with a sliding partition and a big stove in the middle of the room. The toilets were outside, big pine bench with Izal toilet paper.

In 1887, In accordance with a recommendation of Mr Beckett, surgeon, the infant school was closed for a fortnight due to an outbreak of measles. In 1913 a committee was formed to interview Mr A. Fuller regarding a small piece of land in his garden to be used for emptying the privies of the infants' school.

The school closed in the 1960s and the infants joined the new school on Main Street. The building was hired from the Feoffees for use as a

> There was an air raid shelter in the playground and, as I remember, we children had to run down there one day. It consisted of a bench either side so we were facing each other. It was dark and cold.

youth club. It has since been demolished and is marked by a plaque on the gates to the allotments.

There was an air-raid shelter next to the school with benches down either side. When the shelter was demolished the rubble was used to improve the state of Bield Drove.

> I remember that we had to line up two abreast and walk to the "big school" for dinner. It was like a scene from Oliver. Sitting on long lines of bench seats, being dished up food I didn't like and being made to eat it all quickly as we had to line up and walk back to school.

A small lane at the end of Eagles Lane that leads to the allotments is called Anchor Close. A parcel of land at the end of the close was sold to the Rural District Council in 1963 for a sewage pumping plant.

Ely Road, Little Street and Seven Sisters

Maps from the early 1900s show Ely Road to be largely undeveloped between Cannon Street and Little Street and there has been gradual development to form a continuous landscape of homes on both sides of the street. On old Ordnance Survey maps the name Little Street is applied to the general area around the lane that now bears the name as a separate hamlet. It is well remembered locally that the street now known as Little Street was once called Duck Puddle Lane, however this name does not appear in the census or any official documents. I have only found one written reference to Duck Puddle Lane which was in a newspaper cutting.

The row of houses on the west of Ely Road were built as council houses in 1924. In 1951 a row of thirty trees, ten maple, ten almond and ten flowering plum trees were planted between Cowbridge Hall Road and Lawn Lane to commemorate the Festival of Britain. These have had to be replaced on an individual basis as they reach the end of their natural lives but they form a picturesque welcome to the village. The planting was organised by the Parish Council and the trees were supplied by councillor B. Easy. This stretch of land was owned by William Martin in 1844 with a horse pond on the corner of Lawn Lane. He also held the land to the west from the Bishop of Ely. Beyond Cowbridge Hall Road the land was divided into strips with several different owners.

The Windmill

On the corner of Cowbridge Hall Road there is a converted tower

It still had the original stone flag floor, apparently it was bad luck to lift the flags. I remember grandad putting a new roof on it in the late 1970s, he did it all from a series of ladders up the inside.

windmill. There is no mill shown here on the 1844 enclosure map when this parcel of land was owned by Huntingdon Martin and called Old House Close. By 1885 the mill is shown as a windmill (corn) on the edge of Huntingdon Martin's land. The only millers in the parish in 1861 are at Pymoor Lane. In 1871 John

Photo Courtesy
Cambridgeshire Collection

Cornwell, miller, is recorded as a living in Main Street and this was known as Cornwell's Mill.

In 1857 John Cornwell married Frances Lofts, the daughter of John Lofts, a millwright on the 1871 census, so perhaps John Lofts built the mill. By 1881 John Cornwell had become a miller and shopkeeper. John's son, Richman, moved to Haddenham but returned to Little Downham and was later listed as proprietor of the mill although he lived in Main Street. The 1896 Kelly's Directory lists John Cornwell as miller (steam & wind). Richman had several run-ins with the law mainly due to drunkenness. The 1925 Ordnance Survey map lists the mill as disused.

> Mr and Mrs Lockwood who owned the windmill were lovely and always very kind to the children when strawberry picking.

Later on the windmill was owned by Arthur and Marie Spinks who lived at Townsend, they grew strawberries on the land, and in the 1980s and 90s did pick-your-own strawberries. This business was taken on by Don Lockwood. After standing derelict for some years it has been converted into a private residence.

55 Ely Road

The bungalow here is a good illustration of the change of land ownership that has taken place through the years. It is built on land once owned by Woods Green on an area generally known as Hither Beald Field. Woods Green died in 1840 and the land came into the possession of Charles Bidwell who seems to have inherited part of Hither Beald Field in trust in 1887. Charles died in 1923 and the land was sold to Elizabeth Ann Norman of the nearby Victoria House. Elizabeth died in 1929 and Charles Green, the great Grandson of Woods Green bought the land. He sold it in 1961 to Ambrose and

> My nan and grandad lived in Victoria House for a period when my grandad worked at the hatchery. Cliff and Doreen Crane.

Gladys Marriott who built the bungalow that stands here now and is the home of Avril and Graham Hayter-Smith.

Victoria House

This house is built on land once owned by John Grimditch. It was built in 1887 and was the home of Thomas Smith, a retired Deputy Chief Constable at Ely, and his wife Ann Eliza. After the Smiths came James and Elizabeth Norman. James was a retired farmer and owned land nearby, including the plot that was sold to eventually build number 55.

This cottage was later the home for employees at the nearby hatchery, the Cranes and the Buckleys.

Leaford Drive

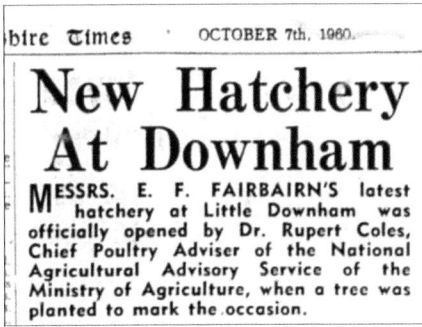

Leaford Drive now stands where there was once a hatchery, opened by E. F. Fairbairn in 1960. At the time it was regarded as one of the largest and most modern in the country and occupied 85 acres. At full capacity, the site could produce approximately 120,000 chicks per week. The company was later taken over by Sterling Chicks.

The hatchery was replaced by Crout's Kitchens with a large house fronting onto the road known locally as the Crout House. The site was then developed as Leaford Drive.

The Spade and Beckett

This detached house on the corner of Ely Road and Little Street was once the Spade and Beckett pub. It first appears in the census returns in 1871 when it was called the Globe and was run by John and Mary Skinner. In 1872 William and Lucy Taylor had taken over. William died in 1886 and Lucy kept the pub herself. At some time between 1881 and 1904 the name changed from the Globe to the Spade and Beckett and in 1904, it was owned by A & B Hall of Ely with Emma still as licensee. The sanitary conveniences were reported as good.

A DOUBLE - FRONTED HOUSE in Ely-road, Little Downham — formerly the "Spade and Beckett" public house—was withdrawn at £1,050 when offered with vacant possession at the White Hart Hotel, Ely, yesterday (Thursday) week, by order of East Anglian Breweries.

The property, set in a small forecourt, contains central entrance lobby wth double doors, front sitting room, another front room formerly used as cellar), front room (formerly tap room), kitchen and pantry. Upstairs are two large and one small bedrooms, all opening on to landing.

Outside are a brick and timber wash-house and garage, urinal, closet, gravelled double-gated entrance from Ely-road, and large enclosed garden with fruit trees and bushes.

Next door to the Spade and Beckett was a house described as a Brick and Tiled dwelling house with two lower rooms and one bedroom, also two lodges, boarded stable and chaff house, cart lodge and a boarded and tiled privy. This house was put up for auction in 1903 by Miss Elizabeth Nicholas.

Isaac Grimditch of Harrow Road, Middlesex son of John Grimditch inherited a messuage or dwelling house in 1883 bounded on the north side by Marshall's Lane and on the West by Ely Road now in the occupation of Daniel Goodwin. He later sold it to Thomas Smith of Ely. There is now a modern bungalow on this site.

Little Street

July 1969: Mr Johnny Brooks of Little Street, Little Downham, one of the last of the threshing tackle operators, helps bag up the last of last season's wheat crop on Mr. Ron Gillett's farm at Little Downham. Behind him is part of his 40-year-old machinery, which is believed to be some of the oldest of its kind left in the country.

Threshing is dying out fast, the stack they did on Mr Gillett's farm "the last of last year's drastic harvest," he says, was probably the only one in the fens to be threshed. The advent of the combine harvester was the beginning of the end for the threshing machine. The other part of Mr Gillett's crop was combined. At 75 Mr Brooks is one of the last in his trade and is probably the oldest man still operating tackle. The fine weather on Thursday enabled him to take one of the few opportunities to practice his trade.

Ernest and Elizabeth Earl and their daughter Ruby lived in a house called The Brambles. Ernest went to court in 1957 when his goat, Clanalpine Bubbles, was attacked by a dog and Ernest was described in a newspaper report as 'white moustached octogenarian', he claimed that he had some of the best goats in England.

> *I can remember Ruby Earl. I used to go down there on a Saturday morning when I was a child and feed her goats (I lived along Ely Road). I always loved the lopped ears ones. She used to make a cup of tea and strain the milk with a muslin cloth.*

Running east from Little Street is Marshall's Lane which, on older maps and census returns, is called Pit House Road. The area to the south of this was called Pit House Field. There is another byway which runs north-south between Marshall's Lane and The Balk variously called Marshall End Road and Pit House Drove. Prior to 1900, there was an agricultural workers cottage on this byway. The census returns also list a house at Chettisham Wood, at one time called Crow Hall and occupied by Christmas Martin, which does not show up on any maps.

A short distance out of the village, just beyond Little Street sits Allotments Farm, on a stretch of road known as Seven Sisters. It is named after seven trees that originally lined the western side of the road and there are many stories about the seven human sisters that they were planted to represent, none of which can be verified. They have been replaced in the past as trees have died and in recent years there were only six. Someone remembers them as at one time being elm trees and there is a story that one was used as fuel in the war. In 2019 they were removed because the ditch on whose banks they sit was dredged exposing the roots and presenting a danger that they would fall into the road. This roadside is now bare and it remains to be seen if they will be replaced. At one end of Seven Sisters, two Byways intersect with the road, heading west is Fox's Drove and going east is The Balk. To the north of Fox's Drove is an area known as Hurst Field and to the north of Balk Drove is Pit House Field.

High Road and Mill Hill

On the 1844 enclosure map, all of the land to the north of High Road (which is then called High Way) was named Mill Piece and was owned by William Martin of Manor Farm with two small sections allotted to Woods Green and John Simpson. The land to the south, known as Clay Way Field, was divided between William Martin, Joseph Vipan and Mary Hammond. By 1923 these sections had become the properties of John Stevens, Charles Bidwell and William Hopkin. Charles Bidwell died in 1922 and a year later his land was up for sale. Charles had rented it out to Owen Charles Few for £25 per year, with outgoings of £5 17s 6d tithe and 1s 6d land tax. The Ordnance Survey maps show that development of the south side of High Road started between 1900 and 1925.

Between Mill Hill and Otterbush, there is a field on the north side of the road that was owned by the Feoffees with a corner of the field labelled as belonging to the Pindars of Downham. A pinder was an official responsible for stray animals and would have been in charge of the pound and this field was let as allotments to raise revenue. In 1966 it was agreed that the church commissioners would offer to sell the pinders allotments to the Feoffees, if the tenants would release the land, it would then be re-let as a single field.

To the left of the pound was Bysouth's top yard, a wood yard, and later, strawberry plugging sheds. Plugging is removing the crown of leaves from the top of the strawberry. People young and old travelled there in the evenings to plug strawberries. A haulage company named T. G. Askew from Wilby used to deliver the fruit to the site and probably remove the end product. The strawberry sheds were replaced by an electronics workshop owned by Pye's of Cambridge.

Pye was for much of the 20th century Cambridge's biggest private employer with at its peak in the 1960s over 7000 staff employed in the Cambridge area and over 14,000 employed in East Anglia. Started in 1896, as a manufacturer of scientific instruments, in the 20s it moved into making radios and in the 30s into making TVs as well. It played a major role in WW2 as the technologies involved in TV translated directly into radar and those in radio into military radio communications. The government put pressure on Pye to move from Cambridge to South Wales where its important work for the military would be less vulnerable. The MD of Pye, C. O. Stanley is reputed to have said 'we are Pye of Cambridge not Pye of Swansea' and refused to move. However, what he did was to set up what became known as the Village Industries. A range of sub-assemblies were 'farmed out' to a wide range of villages across East Anglia to be put together and sent to the main Cambridge factory for final assembly. This local assembly work was carried out in a range of premises, local halls, people's homes and even in a bakery in Sawston. It was estimated that during the war 14,000 people were employed in these Village Industries in East Anglia.

After the war, Pye expanded massively and several of the bigger Village Industries sites became permanent Pye sites usually making components like resistors and capacitors to go into the finished equipment. Examples were at Swaffham and Mildenhall. The site at Little Downham probably shut down in the 1950s but the company retain no records of this facility.

1 and 3 (Apple Tree Cottage) High Road.

Photo Courtesy David Bysouth

The above picture shows two properties, one at the front and one at the back. The building was bought by the Bysouth family who carried out a number of modifications. It was combined to make a single house and later divided again down the middle. The single-storey buildings at the end have now become double-storey extensions and this is now numbers 1 and 3 High Road.

Where number 5 (Daffodil Cottage) now stands Philip Bysouth built a "prefab" cottage made from recycled timber from a chapel in Isleham. It was chicken wire and cement external walls lined internally with plasterboard built on a two brick depth foundation with an asbestos roof.

I believe it was built in the 1930s. Being a prefab it was non-mortgageable. We dismantled it in 2005.

Photo Courtesy David Bysouth

The last reference to mills at Mill Hill are two windmills marked at the top of the hill on Thomas Yeakell's map of 1801. By 1900 there is no trace of them on the Ordnance Survey map.

The cottage sitting on the inside of the bend at the top of Mill Hill was originally made from two old railway carriages that were hauled to the site by cart horses. It was the home of Leslie and May Tutt. Leslie was an airman originally from Brighton and May was the daughter of Arthur Cornwell, a local farmer who lived there before Leslie and May. The railway cottages are now replaced by more traditional building materials but the outline of the carriage roofs are still visible on the inside of the gable walls.

A locally drawn map marks a spot on High Road, just beyond the houses on the south side of the road, as the site of Bronze Age burials found in 1929.

Holme Lane

Holme Lane is not given a name on old maps and has a variety of names on the census returns. The first mention is 1841 when it is called Backside, presumably because it is to the rear of the plots that line Main Street. The name varies between Backside and Back Street until 1881 when Edward Wilson is living in Backside but Isaac Taylor is living in Cross Lane. In 1933 Arthur Gotobed married Audrey Leaford and was recorded as living in Back Lane but it was Cross Lane in 1939 when Percy Green is living at Rye House, Cross Lane. It has been called

Thursday, 12th January, 1967

OP bungalows for Downham and Sutton

A revised sketch scheme for 14 old people's bungalows, warden's accommodation and communal block at Little Downham was accepted by Ely R.D.C. Housing Committee at a meeting on Wednesday of last week. The bungalows — six two-bedroomed and eight one-bedroomed will be built in a quadrangle and situated off Pond Lane.

Cross Lane within living memory (not to be confused with the other Cross Lane) and it was some time after this that the name Holme Lane came into use.

On the corner of Holme Lane and Pond Lane is Holme Close, sheltered housing accommodation, built in the late 1960s.

Rye House is the most notable property in Holme Lane and the land behind it running down to Cannon Street was orchards. The census returns record various inhabitants over the years as gardeners and it seems likely that they were the residents of Rye House making a living growing fruit. The large barn behind the house was an apple store. In 1861 Isaac Taylor, son of Castledine Taylor, was the gardener in Backside until he died in 1886 although his wife Mary remained here in 1891. The Taylors were succeeded by Charles Hull, who in turn was succeeded by Percy Green, son of Charles Green the harness maker, and later associated with Bury House.

Barnhouse is the large apple barn that was originally part of the Rye House estate. Derek and Helen Last bought Rye House and converted the barn in the 1980s into an environmentally friendly project with solar heating, water recycling and a productive garden. They named it Barnhouse. As I write the barn has been bought by new owners and is undergoing further renovation. The interior has been gutted, the small rooms combined into larger ones and an extension is being erected to the rear. The new owner hopes to retain original features and continue with the environmental aspect of the project as much as possible. The most obvious original brickwork is in the base of the east wall and a retaining wall for a ramp at the rear. The new owner is considering a name change for the house.

Lawn Lane, Lawns Crescent and Orchard Estate

As you walk down Lawn Lane from the village green there is a field on the left, often grazed by cows in the summer, with a large drop beyond the hedge. The field belongs to Lawn Farm and is where the ballast was taken to build the railway.

In winter, years ago when we used to get a decent amount of snow, I used to go down the slope on a sled or a plastic fertiliser bag. The bag wasn't too good if not a lot of snow as a bit bumpy and you could get a bruised backside.

The 1844 enclosure map only marks fields to the south of Lawn Lane and the land from Ely Road to the cemetery was owned by William Martin. The cemetery is on Glebe land with a small section in the corner where number 8 is built. This plot and the land beyond the cemetery was owned by Huntingdon Martin with land beyond that owned by Owen Cole and then Cole Bays. Cole Bays' land bordered onto the Brick Kilns which were on land owned by Mrs Mary Martin.

DOWNHAM HIT BY PARAFFIN SHORTAGE.

"Give Us Electricity" Petition to R.D.C.

Among those hard hit by the paraffin shortage are some forty-odd residents of Lawn-lane Council Houses, Little Downham.

They are each able to obtain half a gallon weekly, which, they say, is quite inadequate now the long nights are approaching.

Most of them are farm labourers. They have to get up at five, and in most households artificial light will be needed for two or three hours every morning. This alone will eat up their fuel ration, for there is no gas and no electricity.

So that, after a hard day's toil on the land, they are faced with the prospect of spending their evening leisure hours in rooms dark except for the dim flicker of the fire.

We understand they're going to put their case to Ely Rural Council—with a petition that electricity shall be installed in the houses.

On the 1885 Ordnance Survey map, there are two joined dwellings on the site of number 8 and the cemetery is mapped out. A small building is marked roughly where Orchard Estate emerges onto Lawn Lane and then the bottom third of the South side is taken up by the brickworks. This remains the same until the 1925 map when the buildings at number 2 have changed footprint, numbers 57 to 67 have been built in 1921 and number 69 has also appeared. The brickworks has now ceased operating and the area is covered with small fields mainly used as paddocks. Some of the social housing at the village green end was built in 1937 with the remainder of the housing being built at various dates since then.

In 1993 the even numbers of Lawn Lane were renumbered so that some of the houses which front onto Lawn Lane but were part of the Orchard Estate became part of Lawn Lane. Also as part of the renumbering, the cemetery became number 10 because it has a standpipe and Anglian Water insisted on a number.

2 Lawn Lane

The 1885 Ordnance Survey map shows number 2 with several farm buildings and two dwellings. The deeds to this house go back to the

1920s although the current house is older and there has been a dwelling here since at least the 1840s when it was the only house recorded in the census in Lawn Lane, the home of George and Susanna Hull. George was a gardener and they had a lodger, Thomas Chapman, a carpenter. George was born in 1796, the son of Allen and Elizabeth Hull who may well have lived here before George.

Ten years later four families were living in Lawn Lane including George and family who had now acquired a servant named Ann Lofts and Richard Forman and family, a farm labourer probably living in a cottage attached to the farm at number 2. George died in 1877 and was succeeded as head of the household by his son William who in turn was succeeded by his son Benjamin.

> *I remember going there in the early 1950s and it was old then. No bathroom and an outside loo. It did have electricity but only cold water with a water heater on the scullery wall. While my grandad was alive, and even when Gordon and Elsie lived there, the gardens were well looked after, with a large veg patch over the fence behind the small wooden sheds facing the barn. The area behind the barn towards the road was mainly gooseberry bushes. Grandad kept the orchard, mainly apples with a couple of Victoria plum trees and pear trees. Just beyond the end of the barn was another small shed, used for storing wood, outside of which was an old horse-drawn cart, but I don't remember ever seeing a horse. Grandad had an old car, I think a Ford, which had been cut off behind the front seats and boarded to make a wagon to transport fruit up the orchard to store in the barn. The field beyond the trees down to the lane beyond was let for growing corn, but there was a large area from the top corner down to a five bar gate where grandad grew strawberries. I spent many happy hours there with Gaga, as I called my grandad, and as I got older helped to pick the soft fruit in the summer earning the princely sum of six old pence a bushel.*

In this time the family trade changed subtly from gardener to fruit grower. Benjamin was the father of Lewis Hull who was a well-known shop keeper in Main Street. Benjamin was still living here in 1939 and died in 1943. It then became the home of Lewis and his wife Emma and then Gordon and Elsie Hull, Gordon was the son of

Lewis and at his marriage he was described as a taxi proprietor. The Hull family built the neighbouring bungalow at number 1 Ely Road and members of the family still live there.

The house was let for a number of years in the 1970s and then bought in 1980 by a family called Perrin. The Booths bought it from them in 1982 when it had become run down and was unmortgageable, and the garden was just a field. The Booth family converted outbuildings to become number 4 in 2012.

The Hull family owned the land that the bungalows at 12 and 14 Lawn Lane are built on and also part of the Orchard Estate.

6 Lawn Lane (Pegasus)

Pegasus was another property built by the Hull family and was the home of Lewis' son Donald and his wife Norah.

12 and 14 Lawn Lane

John Jenkins and Tom Handley built 12 and 14 respectively. The Hopkirk family bought number 14 from the Handleys.

Andrew Hopkirk was a physician at the RAF hospital in Ely and remembers his time in Little Downham:

The original owner retained part of his plot to the south-east on which he had a large shed. To the north-east of our garden was a car park, now Orchard Estate, and immediately north a small bungalow on the road. At that time Downham was a thriving but much smaller village than it is now. It had just completed building a village hall when we arrived and this was well used for village events. All residents were expected to attend events and the local hops were always crowded. The vicar was very active in promoting village activities and the church attendance was very high. The primary school thrived under its head teacher Tony Hurlin. We certainly had a very happy time living there.

16 Lawn Lane

This bungalow was built in 1929 by the Hull family and rented out. It was bought from Richard Hull by the Tuck family in 1968

The land for Lawns Crescent was bought by Ely Rural District Council in 1945 from the Ecclesiastical Commissioners for England and the houses built the following year.

Orchard Estate was built in 1950 on land that was originally orchard. Kiln Close was built later and named for the nearby brickworks.

Main Street

1 Main Street

Built in 1850 this house was later owned by George Green of Bury Farm and was probably built as a farmworker's cottage. Ken and Pam Bailey lived here while Ken worked for George Green.

Judy Ball bought the house circa 1980 and it was then bought by its current owners.

2 and 4 Main Street

These two cottages were once barns for the neighbouring lodge and were the first barn conversions in Little Downham. The Cooke family who lived at Lawns Farm and The Lodge also owned these barns. Gwendoline Cooke married Cyril Fendick in 1951 and the Fendick family sold them for seven shillings and sixpence. If you look closely the place where the large barn door was bricked up can be seen.

6 Main Street (The Lodge)

The Lodge was home to the Cooke family in the early 1900s and then the Fendicks, when Gwendoline Cooke, daughter of Arthur

Mason Cooke of Lawns Farm, married Cyril Fendick. Miss Ethel Cooke who had been invalid for many years and was aunt to Gwendoline also lived here.

> When we came to the village in 1982 Mrs Fendick was very kind, she liked to talk to our small children. Kath Parr cleaned for her and a Mrs Lofts, who lived in Eagles Lane, was her gardener and walked the dog.

The railings were removed in the second war as part of the drive to collect metal. The railings have been replaced by the current owners, the Summersgills.

Lawns Farm

Lawns Farm is the last farmyard to access directly onto Main Street. There is a large farmhouse, hidden from view by hedges, and an access road running beside the church to a cottage and outbuildings. A new bungalow has been built on the field fronting onto the road where the village feast used to be held.

In 1851 Huntingdon Martin lived here and was a farmer of 750 acres employing 40 men and 30 children. He had a visitor when the census was taken, Rev George Abrahams

MAY 16, 1924.

ELY PROPERTY SALE.

"The Lawns," Little Downham Under the Hammer.

There was an unusually large attendance at the Public Room, Ely, yesterday (Thursday), when Messrs. Bidwell & Sons, of Ely, offered the freehold farm known as "The Lawns," Little Downham, for sale.

The property consists of 213a. or. 4p., together with an attractive residence, and farm buildings and cottages, now in the occupation of Mr. Arthur M. Cooke, who is terminating his tenancy at Michaelmas, 1924. Included in the sale was an eight-roomed house, with 1a. or. 39p. of pasture land, and 4a. 3r. 37p. of pasture land and garden allotments, the latter in the occupation of Mr. Cooke and the Parish Council respectively.

The bidding for the Lawns Farm started at £6,000, and eventually Mr. George Darby purchased the lot for £8,400. The house and grass paddock went to Mr. Archer for £370, while 4a. 3r. 37p. of pasture and arable land was bought by Mr. A. J. Sennett for £190. The small holding was bought in at £720. 6a. 0r. 38p. of Fen arable land went to Mr. G. Hobbs for £360.

Independent minister of Regent Street Chapel, London. Born in, Prussia, Poland.

By the 1871 census, Mason Cooke had taken over the farm although his landholding was much reduced as he farmed 350 acres employing 13 men and 5 boys. Mason gave up another farm on Main Drove in 1874.

Mason Cooke was succeeded by his son Arthur Mason Cooke who sold the farm in 1924 and it was bought by George Darby for £8,400. A house and grass paddock included in the sale was bought by Mr Archer for £370. In 1942 George's son Francis sold the farm to E. F. and B. C. Harrison for a 'satisfactory price' although Bertram Harrison was already living there in 1939. It included a modern house with a tennis lawn, a homestead and cottage.

At one time it was a dairy and arable farm. The milk was bottled there and delivered to all of Downham and The Droves.

Den Harrison later took over the farm but the fields are now rented out mainly for arable but beef cattle are still kept on two fields. The cattle pasture bounded by Lawn Lane has a large depression where gravel was extracted for building the railway.

A milk bottle from Harrison's Dairy.

At weekends I washed the empty bottles up for pocket money. Still have the scars from the bottles that got broken. I had an idyllic twenty years there.

March 1906 Parish Magazine

One of the most largely attended funerals in recent times was witnessed on 14th February when Mr Mason Cooke was buried and no one probably ever before has been for so many years so consistently and actively connected with parish affairs as he was.

His name first appears in the parish minute book in 1858 and from that time very few meetings were held in the parish which Mr Mason Cooke did not attend. At that time Mr Law was Rector. Mr Fisher was curate. Mr Huntington and Mr William Martin took a very active part in all parish matters.

Strange as it may appear to us now, Mr Mason Cooke assisted in making a Church rate for the repair of the parish church and also a rate for the destruction of sparrows. How many and how rapid have been the changes through which he lived. A man of great personality and strong convictions he always had the courage of his opinions. Neither popularity nor unpopularity was ever allowed to interfere with what he considered the faithful discharge of his duties. For nearly fifty years he took a leading part in the concerns of the parish and until illness, that leveller of all men, laid him low, he worked at public affairs with all the energy of a young man.

Now with a good and long record of activity and integrity of purpose he has gone to his rest. Soon the green grass will be growing over the grave of a man who lived a long life, who was noted for doing all work under his care thoroughly well, who was always upright, known for his puritan sternness and with whom more or less every change in the civil life of the parish was associated.

Of course we cannot help regretting that his views as a pronounced Baptist so often brought him into opposition to the principles and work of the Church. Still with all our hearts we say 'may he rest in peace.

Harrison's Field and the Village feast

There is a field on the corner of Main Street and Church Way, part of Lawns Farm, which is now the site of a modern bungalow. A festival known as the Village Feast was held on the first weekend in June. A Sunday service was held in the evening on the Church Way Green with the village pump (no longer there) serving as the pulpit.

I can remember the fair. I'm sure it was called 'the feast' and I remember the swing roundabout with an old man making it go round and round by turning it by hand from a handle in the middle of the roundabout.

There was a fair that lined Main Street and spilt down the side streets which later became a parade through the village and finished with a feast and fair on the field which was run by Charlie Nunn from March. There were penny slot machines and bric-a-brac stalls.

I remember the village feast, a fair that visited once a year. As a child it felt huge but really only consisted of a small roundabout and sideshows. I remember winning a goldfish there, what joy, absolutely fantastic.

If I remember correctly they would smash two old pianos up!! It all had to go through a small hoop. First to get their piano through was the winner.

I remember the little fair, used to love going there, they had the swinging chairs.

The 1p machines with the ball bearing would fling the ball around the edge and if it landed in one of the holes in the middle you got 1p or 2p or 5p. There was a rifle range where you knocked over the pegs for plaster prizes or coke cans with expanding foam tops. Oh! and oversized £10 notes.

3 and 7 Main Street

This was three homes, number five was to the rear of number seven and the two have been combined, there is now no number five. The houses had become very dilapidated and were renovated in the early 2000s.

In 1953 numbers 3 and 5 were put up for auction by Mrs G. Reditt. Number three was let to Ernest Easy for 10 shillings a week. It was described as follows:

Entrance lobby, sitting room with fireplace and two built-in cupboards, living room with two windows, portable cooking range and pantry, cupboard, store room with lean-to iron roof and two bedrooms.

The original detached house was split into three, there was a huge orchard behind. We still have a few remaining trees in our garden.

Number 5 was vacant and was smaller:

Living room with portable cooking range and built-in cupboard and one bedroom.

Outside there were two brick built wash houses with coppers, coal lodge, two closets (one brick and pantiled, the other timber and iron roofed).

St. Leonard's Church

St. Leonard is the patron saint of prisoners, women in labour and diseases of cattle. The church was built in the 12th century from flint with a stone dressing and has been added to and updated several times since. One of the main treasures of the church is the royal coat of arms which has been described as one the finest in the country. All churches had to have coats of arms from the reign of Henry VIII. This one was painted in 1763 on wooden panels.

The Victorians extended the panels in 1868 and also repainted the arms. In 1973 the arms were again restored, undoing some of the damage done by the Victorian renovations.

The box pews and the gallery where the band would play were also removed.

FRIDAY, **The Cambridgeshire Times** JUNE 16, 1990.

REPAIRS TO LITTLE DOWNHAM CHURCH TOWER.

The photographs which we reproduce above will give readers a good idea of the trouble which was recently reported, and which is now being dealt with, at Little Downham Church. The most serious fall of masonry, or rubble, had already been repaired before the photographs were taken. This repair consisted of a pier of brickwork from the floor level up to the base of the old boarding which bears the Royal Arms, laid in cement and grouted, to a depth of nearly 4 feet. The salient angles of the tower, beneath the supporting baulks of timber, have been underpinned with reinforced concrete to a depth of 10 feet. In the interior surface of the belfry on the first floor level a 'collar' of reinforced concrete is being inserted to prevent the widening of the cracks which had appeared inside and out.

The church clock was built by John Smith of Derby, installed in 1922 and is a five-day clock. It cost £180 with £100 coming from a legacy of Lord Downham, William Hayes Fisher, and the remainder raised from public subscription. It is generally very reliable although there was a problem in the cold winter of 1962/63 when the cogs shrank. Small weights keep the clock going with a large pendulum at the bottom and washers used to regulate the speed. The clock face is gold leaf.

There are recent stories of hauntings in the graveyard. Individuals and groups in medieval clothing have been reported.

We went to church every Sunday and we had a stamp book and got a stamp to put in it to show that you really did go to church.

63

One notable rector was Thomas Jones who married a rich heiress and bankrupted her within three years with bad investments in fenland. In 1777 Jones was imprisoned in the Fleet owing £38,000.

Old Rectory

One of the older houses on Main Street, the Rectory was built for Thomas Waddington, rector of Little Downham between 1787 and 1805. There is a plaque in the west wall inscribed ' TW 1790'. It is built of yellow gault bricks.

There have been stories of hauntings here with a young vicar's daughter reporting supernatural happenings and a workman who attributed a missing cup of tea and his trousers falling down to ghosts.

Rectory

The current rectory sits in what was part of the grounds of the old rectory. In 1926 the Rector, Rev. H. K. Stallard had the stable converted into a Parish Room for the use of parishioners. These were used for functions, Cubs, Scouts and Girl Guides on the right side with toilets and stables on the left side.

There is a postbox in the garden wall, now disused. A wall letterbox was first placed here in 1887 although the current one is from the reign of Edward VII so not the original.

> *These were the days when Rev Suter did a sermon entitled Guiness and Cream Cakes and Bill Patterson converted most of the regulars at the Plough.*

The women's Institute in Little Downham was started by the Rector's wife, Mrs Greenstart in 1918 and meetings were held in the Canning

House situated at the bottom of the rectory garden. Subsequently, an old army hut was purchased for £137 funded partly by the WI with Mr John Stevens of the Manor House donating the rest. The hut was placed in the south-west corner of the rectory grounds next to what is now the entrance to the new rectory.

During the second war, the hut was briefly used as a school for evacuees. It was taken down in the late 1960s.

The kerb stones for most of the north side of Main Street, from Lawn Lane to Eagles Lane, were specially made for Little Downham by Joseph Hamblet, a brickmaker of West Bromwich. They are made of Staffordshire Blue brick and dated 1896.

9 Main Street (Lofts Cottage)

The 1844 enclosure map shows a smaller building with a different footprint on land owned by the Reverend John Henry Sparke. John Henry Sparke was Canon and Chancellor of Ely Cathedral and owned land around Ely and Mattishall in Norfolk. His son, Henry Astley Sparke was a lieutenant in the 4th Light Dragoons and was killed in the Charge of the Light Brigade aged about 27.

Lofts shop circa 1920. *Photo Courtesy Cambridgeshire Collection*

> *Brings back memories, half penny sweets and Mrs Lofts being slightly grumpy.*

This building was originally a row of three cottages owned by Joshua Lofts. His son, Ben, converted them into a single entity as a shop in 1907. Ben Lofts was a well-known character and is remembered for many reasons. He was proprietor of the shop that sold everything for 61 years, eventually being succeeded by his daughter, Eva. In the early days of motoring Ben Lofts was the first person in the village to retail petrol, and he also ran a taxi service. He served as a

> *She used to terrify me when I was younger but always went there for sweets.*

special constable for many years. He also sold paraffin from a barrow that he pushed around the village.

Possessing a deeply religious nature he was a founder member of the Methodist Church in the village and was a Sunday School teacher for 50 years. Loving children, he had an ever-open bag of sweets for his Sunday School scholars. He was for many years closely connected with local sports as chairman of the former Ely and District Football League and chairman of Little Downham's football and cricket clubs. He was also instrumental in forming the now-defunct local bowls club. Many people have a story to tell of the shop as they remember it from their childhood and they often found the place quite scary. There was a wooden bench in the shop and there were sweets and chocolate in the window, which caught the sun, giving the shop the nickname of "Mouldy's".

> *I remember home delivery on a handcart, including paraffin*

> *I loved the smell of the shop and the wooden bench. Dad used to go in to get his veg seeds and Eva used to weigh them out and wrap them in newspaper, and my grandad used to go up there to get his baccy and sweets. You could buy all sorts of stuff that you couldn't find anywhere else.*

After the shop closed it was bought by Richard, an Architect, and Phyllis Ambrose. The property was quite run down and the upstairs was accessed by ladder. They named it Lofts Cottage in remembrance of the Lofts family.

> *My nan said that, during the war, Ben Lofts used to send a rumour around the village that he may have 'a few tomatoes' in the shop the next day. Well he never had any tomatoes but he did have a shop full of customers.*

Village Hall

The original building was constructed in 1779 on the site of the former Guildhall as a boy's school and workhouse.

The first headmaster was George Langman who was paid ten pounds a year to teach 24 boys. Records show that there had been an earlier school in the parish founded in 1582 when George Archer was licensed to teach but the site is unknown.

In April 1865 Rev Fisher reported on the crowded state of the school with 90 boys and 70 girls. This resulted in a proposal to enlarge the school and separate boys and girls and in 1886 the workhouse section was altered to become the girl's school.

The school was regularly inspected by the education authorities and in 1878 the Feoffees received the following comments:

Boys School: The upper part of the school is well taught. The lower part shows need for additional teaching. Mr Aspland is a competent and conscientious teacher but the school is too large for him to teach adequately with such weak assistance as he at present has. A classroom is much needed.

Girls School: This school is in very good order and the upper part of it is well taught, that the lower part is in need of a stronger staff is very apparent. Mrs Cole is a very efficient teacher in a school of this size. At least one pupil teacher is needed for. A classroom is much wanted.

In December of 1884 the Feoffees wrote to the education authority in a bid to improve the inspection results:

I am requested by the Feoffees to represent to the education department that the time of year appointed for the examination of Downham and Pymoor schools by H M Inspector is inconvenient and unsuitable. This being a very extensive and purely agricultural parish consisting of nearly 10,000 acres, many of the children are sent by their parents to work in the fields in the summer time. The consequence is that when the inspector visits the school in June many of the children are absent. Even when it is possible to bring the children out of the fields to be presented for examination, it is too often found that they have forgotten much of what they have learnt. Thus in the examination the children do not do justice to the instruction which they have received, the report of the school suffers in consequence and the grant is diminished. Under these circumstances the Feoffees would be grateful to their lordships if they could see their way to change the date of the examination from June to February or March in order that more satisfactory results may be obtained.

This request was refused.

There was much debate on what should be taught and what books should be available resulting in the following motion:

That the Downham Feoffees School should be kept perfectly unsectarian, and with regard to the religious training of the school, the bible alone be read and taught, also that the children shall not be called upon to attend church on saints days without the sanction of the Feoffees.

The Feoffees voted on this motion: 3 for, 1 against, 3 abstained.

The Feoffees agreed in 1914 that the school could be used as a military hospital if required.

In July 1922 Mr Crabbe asked for use of the Bier House as a bicycle store for school children who currently used Mr Green's yard. The Bier had not been used for several years and it was agreed that it should be sold and the proceeds given to the cemetery fund. It is not clear exactly where the bier house was located but it was possibly in the grounds of the rectory.

I remember the school when it was double height with the dormer windows. There were three classrooms divided by very tall, heavy folding doors and the classroom on the right had a stage, used by teachers for morning assembly and the Christmas concert.

The building remained in use as a school until the 1960s and after standing empty for some time, the building underwent substantial renovation and was converted into the Village Hall, which opened in 1974, 'for the use of the inhabitants of the Parish of Little Downham in the County of Cambridge and Isle of Ely . . . with the object of improving the conditions of life for the said inhabitants'. Taken directly from the Conveyance dated 25th October 1972. Since then a lot has gone on including a new kitchen and up-dated Stage lighting and sound system.

It is also now the home of the Book Cafe, a volunteer library although it is not allowed to use the name library by Cambridgeshire Library Services as part of the agreement that allows the Book Cafe to access Cambridgeshire Libraries books and services.

10 Main Street

Originally this was the schoolmaster's house owned by the Feoffees. In 1911 it was inhabited by Lionel Sedly who had a boarder called Frederick Groom. Both are described as headmaster, elementary school.

In 1912 the house was in a bad condition and it was reported that it was difficult to employ a headmaster because of the poor state of the accommodation on offer. Two solutions were initially considered, rebuilding the current house or finding a site for a new house. A proposal was made to build a new house in School Lane behind the existing schoolmaster's house but it was thought that this would not leave sufficient space for a garden for either property.

It was eventually decided to rebuild the existing house at a cost not exceeding £300 and a quote of £147 from F. Hobbs of Downham was accepted. In 1918 Mr and Mrs Crabbe were appointed schoolmaster and schoolmistress and moved into the house. They were still there in 1939.

The last schoolmaster to live here was Mr Ives. After this, it was the home of Ernie and Pearl Wiltshire.

Derek and Gillian Harrington moved here and converted part of the house into a butchers shop.

The 1900 Ordnance Survey map marks the Post Office as being at the end of School Lane and the 1901 census lists George Aspland as sub-postmaster

Mr Ives was headmaster at 'Top School' as we called it and Sheila Sole was one of the teachers. They were both brilliant teachers.

living next to the school with his brother Alfred as a postman. Feoffees minutes also refer briefly to maintenance of the post office. It therefore seems likely that this house was briefly the post office before it moved along the Main Street to Sennitt's shop.

71

From the Parish Magazine July 2012

11 Main Street (Bury House)

This is reputedly the oldest house in the village and was the farmhouse for Bury Farm which is now Bury Green. There is a stone plaque on the east wall stating 'RC 1700' and there are 19th and 20th-century renovations.

It is partly made from material from the demolished Bishop's Palace. It has two storeys, attics and cellar with an original lobby entry which was sealed circa1900 when the main entrance was moved and the porch built. There is an extension at the back which is clearly of a later date to the original building. When the Ambrose family bought the house the upper part of this extension was being used as an apple store which has now been knocked through to the main house and is a bedroom.

On the 1861 census John Newton, farmer of 250 acres employing 7 men and 3 Boys lived here. By 1881 Jonathon Norman, farmer 390 acres employing 9 men and 3 boys had moved in.

By 1939 the farm had been taken over by George Green who lived here with his wife Grace and George was succeeded by Percy Green. The house was bought from the Green Family by Richard Ambrose who carried out further modifications and restoration and his family still live here. The farm was sold for development and is now Bury Green and Matthew Wren Close.

There is a Latin inscription carved into the fireplace which translates as follows:

The man serves thee who adjusts to time.

He will serve thee who will come to time.

This is another house that has stories of ghosts with windows being mysteriously opened.

13 Main Street (Flanders House)

First identifiable on census returns in 1891 this was the home of William Flanders, a farmer, born in Wimpole but from a Little Downham family, who married Ann Eliza Hopkin, a local girl. In 1951 Frederick Flanders and Hilda Davidson, administrators of the will of Sarah Rebecca Flanders (spinster), sister to William, sold it to Grace Green (wife of George Woods Green) of Bury House for £1400. The garden extended to Cannon Street and the conveyance includes dwelling house, farm premises, yard, garden and paddock.

Total area of three roods thirty-two poles (more or less) with a frontage of fifty-eight feet on Main Street and fifty-six feet on Cannon Street.

Derek John Hills bought it from John Beckett (deceased) 1976 for £8000 and Colin and Yvonne Hills bought it from Derek Hills in 1984.

15 Main Street (The Old Forge)

Next to the house was the site of the blacksmiths forge belonging to William "Billy" Saberton although William lived in Cannon Street and the business was later taken on by his son Frank. Frank had a reputation for strong and loud language. The forge was opposite the school and the children sometimes had to be

> We found a lot of blacksmith iron ore in the footings. The horse latches and hooks are still on the side of the house.

encouraged to sing in order to limit their exposure to the tirade from over the road. The forge was closed when the business moved to Cannon Street in 1961 and was taken on by Frank's son Peter.

The house was originally two properties. In 1901 Little Sallis Lofts lived in the house next to the forge and the Smith family, who were farmers, lived next door. Little Sallis Lofts was a school assistant who spent some time travelling in America. He claimed to have taken part in the civil war but the dates for the civil war and his age don't quite coincide. In the 1930s another Smith, Harry, bought the two houses and combined them. Harry Smith sold the property to the owners of Bells Coaches who demolished the forge so that the coaches could access the yard at the back.

Two bungalows have now been built in the yard behind the house.

17 Main Street

This cottage was also owned by Harry Smith. It is a late 16th-century building but encased in later brickwork. It was originally thatched and then roofed with corrugated iron which in turn was replaced with old pantiles in 1981.

In the 1940s this was the home of Bert and Olive Bye and later, in the 1970s, it acquired the name of Angel Cottage and Margaret Haynes lived here.

19 Main Street

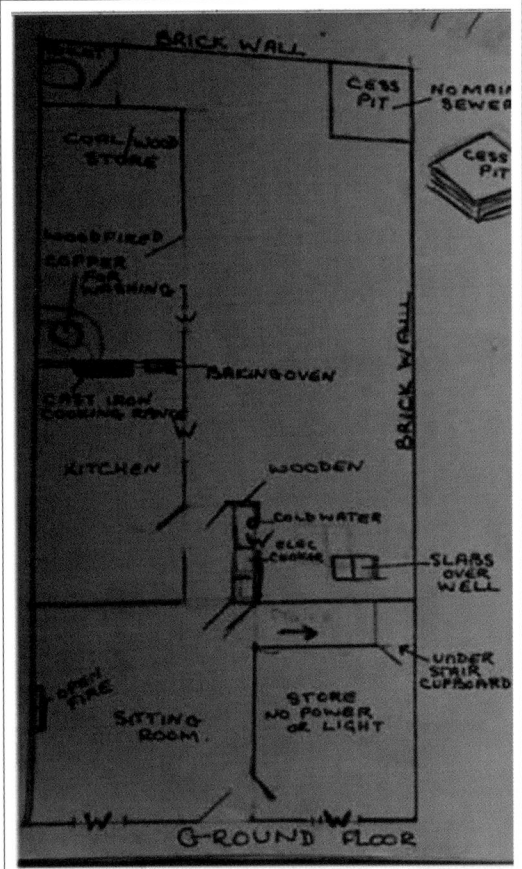

Plan drawn from memory c1995 by
Vivian Haylock.

Again Harry Smith owned this property and it was used as accommodation for his farm workers. The Hull family lived here in the early 1950s when it became vacant but they had to move out when it was once again needed by farmhands. It was sold in the 1960s and became the home of the Barnes family. It was sold on again, underwent substantial renovation and is now owned by the Clark family.

There was a well in the back garden in the 1950s. I remember my mum using the water to fill the copper in the outhouse to do her washing.

Feoffees School

There was a large old house on this site demolished to make way for the school. Approval for building the school was given in December 1965 and the school was opened in 1967/68.

The 1844 enclosure map marks this property as belonging to Daniel Jones and he is living here as a farmer in 1841. Daniel was born in Wales but married Isabella, the widow of Francis Tingey. Daniel also owned a parcel of land at Little Street adjacent to land owned by William Tingey and it seems likely that Daniel came into land through his marriage to Isabella.

The Chestnuts   *Photo Courtesy Cambridgeshire Collection*

The large old house on this site was known locally as the Fretwell House after the Fretwell family although their association with this house appear cursory, the actual name of the house was The Chestnuts. In 1911 William Fretwell, a retired miller from Norfolk, and his unmarried daughters, Etheldreda and Elizabeth, were visiting Walter Wallis and his wife in Pymoor. In 1939 Walter was living here with Elizabeth as his housekeeper. Walter had donated some land from the estate for a war memorial club shortly after World War One so he must also have owned this property when he was farming at Pymoor.

Walter died in 1940 and bequeathed property to Elizabeth in his will including the house referred to as The Chestnuts. Following Elizabeth's death in 1962, aged 90, the Isle of Ely Education Committee made the decision to purchase the house and grounds as the site for the new school.

Elizabeth rented the house out and a later resident was Arthur 'Jammy' Strevons, so-called because he was the general manager of the Ely Jam Factory. The Few family and the Smith family also lived here briefly.

There are memories of it being old and having a wine cellar as it fell into dereliction.

The Institute

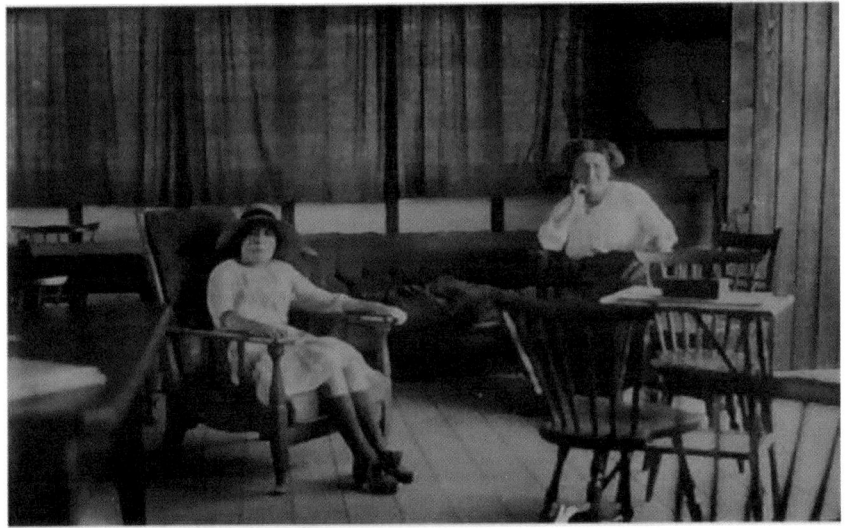

Photo Courtesy Cambridgeshire Collection

As a memorial to World War One, it was proposed to erect a men's club. It would have a reading room, billiards room and a place for meetings. It was to be paid for by public subscription and the site was donated by Mr Walter Wallis. Initially, it was proposed that the Feoffees provide a site in School Lane, which they had agreed to do on a 99-year lease.

An army officers hut from Cambridge was bought for £400 and it cost a further £100 to transport and place it on brick foundations. It was opened in 1919 by Mr C. Bidwell.

This was a prefabricated building in the south-west corner of what is now the school playground (opposite the Anchor pub). During the second war, it was the headquarters of Little Downham Home Guard and was taken down at some time after the war.

21 Main Street (Fitzballe House)

The 1844 enclosure map marks this plot of land as belonging to C. Finch.

This was at one time referred to as the Clergy House and was the residence of the clergy of St Leonard's. In 1871 Nicholas Isaac Hill Fyson lived here. He was the curate at St. Leonard's and was the son of Robert Fyson, a surgeon at Newmarket. Nicholas went on to become the long term Rector of Boylestone, Derbyshire where he died in 1923 aged 82.

In 1891 two members of the clergy lived here. Robert Miles Stapylton went on to be Rector of various parishes in Cambridgeshire, Devon and Yorkshire and John Roper Cooke who went to work in Calcutta. There was also a caretaker here with his wife, John Thomas and Mary Russell.

Albert and Laura Saberton, who started A. L. Saberton Potato Merchants, bought the house at auction in 1936 from the Taylor family who emigrated to America and the Sabertons still run a potato merchants business from here.

The Garage

Photo Courtesy Tony Summersgill

The 1886 Ordnance Survey map shows this site as undeveloped and the garage buildings appear on the 1900 map. The business was being run by George Saberton and Cecil 'Toot' Young (actually Alfred Cecil Young) in the mid-1900s. They also ran a bus, usually driven by Toot, which took people to market each Thursday and Saturday. It seated about 20 people but sometimes carried 30 or more, especially the last one on a Saturday evening after the pubs and cinemas had shut. They also did days out on summer Sundays to places such as Whipsnade and Hunstanton, these were driven by Noble Lely.

George's cousin, Albert Leslie Saberton (the business is still called ALS), bought the business around 1956 although George continued to work there. It was later taken over by Harry Lock in about 1968 and today is owned by Tony Summersgill.

23 Main Street

There is a house shown on this site on the 1886 map but on the 1900 map the shape has altered so this may have been a new building or the house was extended.

In 1939 this was the home of George Saberton who started the garage business. George was the son of William John Saberton, a blacksmith from a family of blacksmiths. George's brother, Hubert, was an apprentice coachbuilder so this may have lead George into the motor trade. This house is now owned by Tony Summersgill.

The Anchor

Landlords of the Anchor	
1871 - 1877	Robert Jordan
1877 - 1913	William Crane
1913 - 1927	Eddy Green
1927 - 1945	William Moore
1945 - 1952	Levi Armsby
1952 - 1960	George Warren
1960 - 1974	Aubrey Davies
1974 - 1977	Brian Bluett
1977 - 1986	Peter Wright
1986 - 2003	Mick Chilvers
2003 - 2008	Jeff Cheeseman

An early mention of the Anchor is in 1808 when landlord Daniel Russell seeks redress from W. Tingay for getting his daughter, Elizabeth, pregnant and was awarded £60.

In 1904 the Anchor was owned by F. L. Harlock, a brewery in Ely. It had stabling for two horses and six vehicles.

Before the recent modernisation by the current owner, Tony Summersgill, there was a room at the back that was used as the village morgue.

Dad took over from Peter Wright. Dad always said that the stables were haunted. I remember him decorating it and a W kept appearing on the wall. Dad could be a bit of a joker.

Somebody told us that the last person to be laid out there when it was the morgue was called Walter.

24 to 30 Main Street

These are Feoffees properties and stand on the site of a row of thatched cottages, also owned by the Feoffees, that fronted directly onto the pavement. In 1912 a proposal was made to pull these down to provide space for a new schoolmaster's house but this was built elsewhere. The Feoffees tenants were living here rent-free. In 1919 the thatch needed repair to make them rainproof and Mr Young (the thatcher who lived over the road at number 27) said that it would need two loads of straw at a cost of £12. The Feoffees tried to negotiate a price of £6 but Mr Young said that more harm than good would come of it for that price and so the Feoffees agreed to £12.

Photo Courtesy Cambridgeshire Collection

They were eventually knocked down in 1936 and there were proposals to build rent-free almshouses to replace them. However, this was not permitted within the scope of the charity and so the plans for two pairs of cottages to be built in School Lane were transferred to this site. A tender of £11,000 was accepted from Percy

Fincham. In 2020, two of these cottages have just been extended and modernised.

27 Main Street

This old thatched cottage was befittingly the home of the Young family, a family of thatchers, and was at one time known as the Thatched Cottage. The grade II listing states that it is possibly late 16th-century and that the Anchor may be built on part of the original building. The first Young recorded here was Isaac Young and his wife Ann, who moved here from a house near the Fox and Hounds, further along Main Street. Isaac's father, Wright Young, was also a thatcher. Isaac and Ann lived here until Isaac died in 1906 and his son, Charles, became head of the household. Charles' wife, Emily, nee Davey, was a teacher. Cecil 'Toots' young, son of Charles and Emily was a motor engineer and he became a partner in the nearby garage business. Cecil's daughter, Cicely, still lives here.

PRETTY WEDDING AT LITTLE DOWNHAM.

Charming Scenes at St. Leonard's Church.

SIMSON—YOUNG.

Considerable local interest was evinced in the marriage at St. Leonard's Church, Little Downham, on Saturday morning, of Mr. Ernest W. Simson, only son of Mr. and Mrs. E. E. Simson, of 41, West-green-road, Tottenham, and Miss Dorothy W. Youngs, second daughter of Mr. and Mrs. Charles Young, of Thatched Cottage, Main-street, Little Downham.

When a liner was put down the chimney of the Anchor during the recent renovations it came out in the fireplace of number 27 so the two buildings are partially linked.

29 - 31 Main Street (Shops)

The row of three units here was built by the Co-op in 1955 on land remembered as derelict at the time. Old maps and photographs show houses built on this site. The 1844 enclosure map attributes ownership of the land to J. Waxham.

New Co-op Shops at Downham

Part of Local Expansion Scheme

The Co-op opened a butcher's, a haberdashery and a grocery as part of the expansion locally of the Co-op into several villages around Ely. When the Co-op closed their operation one of the units was sub-let to serve as the village library.

Other businesses that have operated out of these units are:

Bakery: Mrs Gooden

Fishing tackle shop

Indian restaurant and take away

General store

Tool shop: Proto Tools run by Jack Dickins.

Green Grocer

Hairdresser

Sports shop: Benwick Sports

Carpet shop: David Rosson

Hardware store

> The school used to take us to watch bread and rolls being made around Easter.

> My mum was the manager of the Co-op and Mrs Crane used to run the library when that was in action.

> They had a rifle range to the left of the shop to try out the air rifles. I could never afford one but I used to make out I was buying one just to play.

> The fishing tackle shop used to also sell pet food and bedding. I used to go in there for rabbit food and supplies.

32 and 34 Main Street

These too are Feoffees houses.

At one point Hubert Culpin lived at number 32 and he had been the landlord of the Spade and Beckett in Ely Road. Later Raymond and Judith Sears and family lived here.

Elias King and his wife Hager lived at number 34 until they died within days of each other in 1978.

33 Main Street

Where the new house now stands used to be Harry Lock's yard, Harry owned the garage and this yard was part of the business. Prior to Harry Lock, Percy Green owned the land and donated the site for the new British Legion club which was started but never finished because of lack of funds. This cutting is from 1956.

Downham B.L. builders

START ON NEW HEADQUARTERS

WHAT has for many years now been a dream of members of the Little Downham and Pymoor branch of the British Legion, is just beginning to materialise into something substantial. It is the erection at Little Downham of their own headquarters.

This is being built by members themselves in their spare time, and it stands back off Main-street.

On Tuesday evening, as an added start to the building, the public were invited to help with the foundations by contributing to funds and laying a brick.

FUNDS LOW

Although branch funds are very low a start has been made on their headquarters, with a hope that in the near future they will have enough money to complete the job. To try and achieve this it is planned to hold various functions, at which it is hoped the public will give their full support.

The plans of the building were passed in January, and work on the fundation commenced a fortnight ago. Materials are being bought by the branch, and the cement mixer they are using has been kindly loaned by Major F. G. Stockdale, of Little Downham.

Meetings and functions at present are held in the Women's Institute Hall, but it is hoped to have the new building completed by September.

DIMENSIONS

It will be 60ft. in length and 19ft. 7in. in width, with a height of 8ft. The foundations consist of a 4½in. brick wall of four course, on top of which is to be erected a "Uniseco" hut. Inside it will comprise a hall with a bar and kitchen at the far end, at which in another section will also be the toilets and conveniences.

The entrance to the building will be through double swing doors, and the floor of the hall will be of smooth cement, which may later probably be covered with another material. Heating will come from two combustion burners. So far the colours for the exterior and interior have not been decided.

Among the equipment to be installed will be darts, chess and other items for the benefit of members, of which at present there are about 80, which includes veterans of the first world war.

Apart from the building itself it is planned to convert the frontage for the use of parking cars, and the strip of land running along the side of the building most likely into flower gardens.

36 and 38 Main Street

Again these are Feoffees houses and the inscription on the front suggests that they were built by the Feoffees in 1813 and it names William Martin and John Hopkin. Originally these

were four dwellings, two rooms top and two bottom at the front and the same at the back.

Ethel Covell (later Ethel Lock) and family lived in number 36 from 1960 until she died in 1999.

Number 38 was like this when Christopher and Melinda Woodroffe moved there in 1963. Christopher had been a farmer living in West Fen. He died in 1965, Melinda stayed here until she died in 1992. There are many fond memories of Mrs Woodroffe 'Woody' and she was a favourite with the local children. Melinda washed her hair in rainwater that she heated on a paraffin stove, she had a mangle in the shed for wringing out the washing and she kept jugs of soft water standing in the bath. Mrs Woodroffe didn't have a fridge or a freezer just a pantry and cooked on paraffin stoves. Later on, she did have a two-ring tabletop cooker but no central heating. There was an electric copper and she would do her washing in that on Mondays with condensation running down the walls.

Woody was our Sunday grandma. She was a star. I think different children visited on different days.

In 1955 a complaint was received from Mrs A. Grindrod of 36A Main Street that she did not like climbing the ladder to the bedroom. In 1956 the front and rear sections of 36 were combined to make a single property. It is not recorded when 38 and 38A were combined.

35 to 39 Main Street

Originally four cottages there are now only three with two of them having been combined. In 1945 Annie Mann bequeathed them to her daughter Ada Muriel Cornwell. The deeds refer to the properties as being bounded on the south-east by Cross Lane and on the north-east by Pit Lane.

We have a document that shows the transfer of mining rights from the Church of England.

Ada and her husband, Herbert Cornwell, lived in number 39. Later it was owned by David Anderson, a teacher, and was then bought by

Paul, head teacher at Downham Feoffees School, and Patti Quant. The Wright family bought the house from the Quants.

Number 37 was owned by Lewis Hull who bequeathed it to his granddaughter, Vivian, who sold it in 1975.

40 Main Street

It is remembered that at some time this property was a cobbler's shop along with number 42.

— July 18th/19th, 1968 —

Re-numbering

Houses in Cannon-street and Chapel-street, Little Downham, are to be re-numbered under a scheme approved by Ely Rural District Council last Wednesday.

The re-numbering has been made necessary by the erection of new houses and proposed developments, said the Chief Public Health Inspector, Mr. D J Gwynn.

It can be difficult to locate the position of modern houses in relation to the position of houses referenced in old documents.

41 Main Street

The grade II listing for this building states that it dates from the late 17th century. The 1844 enclosure map shows that this parcel of land was owned by William Cole Bays who married Alice Hopkin in 1823. In 1841 William was a farmer but by 1861 he was a railway labourer living in Islington and subsequent ownership of the land is unknown until the mid-1900s.

Henry Thompson went to the sale of 41 and 43 but Bert Harrison outbid him. Number 43 had a sitting tenant, Mr Ben Philips. Eventually, the two properties were combined to make number 41.

42 Main Street

Minnie Graham is recorded as living here in the 1939 register and she paid for a stained glass window in the church.

Minnie Graham went to court over possession of a house that she had purchased. It is not possible to determine exactly which house that she bought at that time but it is said that she moved into the village from the fen and is not remembered as living anywhere else in Main Street. Therefore this story probably refers to number 42.

Miss Minnie Graham, a school teacher of Main Drove, applied for possession of a house which at the time was occupied by Mrs Herbert Hopkin. Miss Graham said that she purchased the house before Lady Day 1919 from Charles Green, a harness maker, and served Mrs Hopkin with a notice to quit in 1920, the annual rental being £9. When she bought the house the garden was in good condition, well cultivated and planted with bushes and trees. Now pigsties were built where the trees and bushes were. The brick-built store adjoining the house, where she had intended to make a pantry, was now used for storing pig food and she noted ten pigs in the garden, although she understood that there had been more over the last winter. The principal room in the house had previously been used as a shop but was now full of rubbish and cobwebs. The magistrates decided that the notice to quit served on Mrs Hopkin was bad and the case dismissed.

44 Main Street (Humble Spud)

It is thought that this was originally a single-storey cottage, which is now the kitchen and dates to about 1770. In the 1860s or '70s, the front two stories were added along with a second story to the rear.

> When I went to top school in the early 1950s Thompson's sold sweets. Miss Tomtitt, as she was known, would bite a sweet in half to make the weight come right.

The shop in the picture is Thompson and Son, Family Grocer and the business was started in the 1870s by James Thompson, in the 1950s the shop was run by a Miss Thompson. Prior to that, it was Green's Butchers.

Photo Courtesy Alan Newark

Thompson's sausages were famous in the village. A family story has it that Tom Thompson died without passing on the recipe for his award-winning sausages.

The Glover family lived here in the 1960s and early '70s. It became a pottery shop in 1976 belonging to Alan Newark who named it the Humble Spud.

There is a first-floor door visible on the side elevation and it is thought that this was for wheat to be hauled up that was then threshed on the first floor.

45 Main Street

Old photographs show a small fence around the front of numbers 45 and 47. Gwyneth Lupson lived at 45 from 1987 until 2005.

46 and 48 Main Street

An advert for the sale of the Live and Let live in 1865 states that this land was owned by John Stevens. These two houses were built in 1915 by Henry Thompson who lived in number 44.

In the 1970s Mr and Mrs Mott lived in number 46.

Number 48 was bought by the Larks in 1967 for about £400. After this, it has been the home of the Harley family, the Wright family who were builders and extended the property in 1980, the Gilbey family and, currently, the Robbins.

47 Main Street

Avis and Cresswell Crane lived here in the late 1900s and they added an extension. It had an outside toilet with several outbuildings and the walls were originally made of straw but were rebuilt at around this time.

The Kynaston family moved here in 2012 and took down the outbuildings but kept the washroom back wall, floor and fireplace as a feature.

49 (Two Butts Cottage) to 55 Main Street

This row of houses stand on the site of the single-storey outbuilding on the side of number 57 and two single storey thatched cottages. Grace Thompson owned this row of properties.

Herbert and Dorothy Burgess lived at number 55 from the mid-1930s until 1987 and Fred and Elizabeth Crane were their neighbours at 53 for some of that time.

50 Main Street (Live and Let Live)

The first recorded landlord of the Live and Let Live was Uriah Jordan. He was resident there when he bought it at an auction held at the Fox and Hounds in 1865. It was described as a beerhouse with shop and cottage adjoining, with a barn and outbuildings, a yard and productive gardens containing altogether 1 rood and 30 poles. Mr Jordan made several court appearances for failing to produce his licence, letting his horse stray on the highway, opening outside hours and indecent behaviour towards Charlotte Omenta.

Uriah went bankrupt in 1881 but remained as licensee until 1887 although the premises were again sold at auction in 1885. This time it was described as a modern built beer house with a large taproom, cellar, bake-office, grocer's shop, outbuildings, offices and yard. At the time Uriah Jordan was under notice to quit. After Uriah Jordan, the licence briefly went to Frederick Smith, then to James Palmer and in 1904 James Palmer was the owner and licensee, he sold it in the 1920s.

Between July 1923 and July 1924 the pub sold 30½ barrels 216 half-pint bottles, 234 pint bottles and 571 crates of 4-quart bottles. No beer was sold after July 1924. In 1926 James Palmer said that he had sold the premises for £800 and that they were now partly used as a general store.

It then became the home of Harry and Stella Stevens and subsequent owners were Trevor Taylor and Nigel Bailey. During this time there were pigsties in the back garden. In 1969 it was bought by the van

Hellenburg Hubar family who painted the 'Live and Let Live' tiles in the porch. Subsequently, it has been the home of the Evans and then the Wright families.

When the house was put up for sale in 1996 it was called Pyecroft.

52 Main Street (Brackley House)

The 1844 enclosure map marks this property as belonging to Woods Green (part of the Green family who lived at Bury Farm, the Windmill pub and the Harness makers shop) although by this time Woods had moved to Bedfordshire. An advert for the sale of the Live and Let live in 1865 states that this property was owned by Robert Green, Woods' grandson.

By 1911 William Saberton, a blacksmith had moved here from School Lane. Later on, William was described as a farmer, livestock was kept in the yard and there was a well in the cellar from which they pumped water for the animals.

Hairdressers

This small, single-story building, has previously been a potato merchant's, cobbler's and a butcher's shop (there are still meat hooks in the loft). There are memories of it being a wet fish shop run by Mr Smith, who also had a mobile fish van, a converted bus which went around the village.

It may also at one time have been the home of the housekeeper from Brackley House next door.

Suzanne Smith ran the hairdresser's in the late 80s and 90s and it is now run by Dawn Harris.

54 Main Street

in 1911 it was the home of Richman Cornwell, farmer and miller, and his wife, Isabella. By 1939 Richman had retired but maintained ownership of the property and when he died in 1947 he was described as living at the Post Office. The property was put up for sale in 1949 with the following details:

The shop, house, shedding and yard are let to Mrs N. U. Williams under a monthly tenancy at 10/- per week and the cottage and garden are let to Mr R. R. Cornwell under a weekly tenancy at 5/- per week.

Outside: Lodge, 2 closets (1 with Elsan) 2 open sheds, partly demolished piggery, cart shed and barn, tank on brick pier.

The post office continued to operate, run by Mr and Mrs Williams and then their son-in-law Les Bourne. The shop also sold sweets and closed in the mid-1960s when the Post Office moved to the other side of the street.

In 1909 Richman had a brush with the law:

At the Ely Petty Sessions, Richman Cornwell, of Little Downham, was summoned for being drunk and disorderly. P.C. Challis stated that on Boxing Day he heard some shouting near the Windmill public house. He went up to the defendant, who said he had lost his cap. He was the worse for drink. Near the Fox and Hounds the defendant fell down and pulled the witness on top of him. The witness took him home by force and he made a disturbance in his own yard for quite an hour.

In 2001 there was a conveyance between Mr Graham Davies (purchasers) and Mr Dennis Perrin (Vendors).

Photo Courtesy Lorraine Taylor

There are some interesting markings preserved on an interior beam, these may be apotropaic marks for protection against witches.

56 Main Street

Frank and Mary Flude lived here from the late 1960s until 2002.

57 Main Street

This was the home of the Flanders family in the middle 1900s, another family who kept pigs in the back garden. The house was extended in the 1980s and originally the stairs were opposite the front door. The 1925 Ordnance survey map shows a single storey building attached to the left of the house and this is visible in old photos. This has now been replaced by the neighbouring houses.

58 (Millers House) - 62 Main Street

Numbers 60 and 62 were combined to make a single property. Henry Lythell the butcher used to live in 62.

In the 1960s Terry and Elaine Flude lived at number 58 and Elaine ran a hairdressing salon from the house.

These cottages were owned and let out by Grace Thompson and when Grace died in 2008 they were bought as buy-to-let investments and updated. At this time number 58 was named Millers House as it was thought by the new owner to be the residence of a miller who worked the windmill in Ely Road.

59 Main Street (Blush Bridal Shop)

The picture below of a general stores was taken in 1910. Before that, it was a chemist shop run by Robert Blows who married Sarah Brittain. Sarah inherited it from her mother, Elizabeth in 1869. Elizabeth (nee Waddelow) inherited it from her father-in-law, Joseph Brittain, who bought 59, 61 and 63 in 1823. Robert and Sarah Blows only daughter, Elizabeth, married Arthur Sennitt who lived at Vine House.

Photo Courtesy Valerie Watson

Robert Blows was in trouble with the law in 1889. It later became Garners, continuing as a general store for two generations until Jim Garner retired.

Robert Blows, shopkeeper, Little Downham, was summoned for selling gunpowder to a child under 16 years of age, on Nov 5th. Defendant was allowed to pay the costs, 14s, and advised to register his name. He said he would not sell any more gunpowder.

This shop remained a general store for many years and served as the post office for some time owned variously by Ken Gibson, the Reeces and Jeff and Shirley Starling. It was bought by Mr and Mrs Barlow in 1975.

It was my job on a Saturday morning to go and get the bread once Thornhills had made the delivery and spend my 10p.

It was then bought along with the now village shop by a family who amalgamated the two businesses and closed this shop in the 1990s.

The shop remained empty for many years until it reopened briefly as a cake shop and deli in 2013 but only lasted for about a year. It is now Blush Bridal shop run by the Easey family.

They used to sell all kinds of things – sweets in jars behind the till that you bought by weight. You could hire VHS videos, gift/homewares, food, post office at the back. It was a great shop.

There is a small cottage to the rear of number 59, accessed via Holme Lane, which was the home of the Woodbridge family.

61 to 63 Main Street

Joseph Brittain bought 59, 61 and 63 in 1823 and, through marriage, they passed into the Sennitt family who rented them out.

Mrs Connie Harrison lived in 61 for a few years.

64 Main Street (Alpha Cottage)

Alpha Cottage is drawn on the 1900 Ordnance Survey map as a row of three terraced houses. Initially, two of the properties were amalgamated and internal inspection shows evidence of the remaining single cottage in the form of the recess for the front door and the space for the staircase. Later the third cottage was incorporated to make a single dwelling.

Philip Bysouth lived here renting it for seven shillings a week from Miss Stevens when the family moved to Little Downham in 1935. When they moved in it had three front doors, three back doors and two staircases. In the back garden there was a bakers oven. The Bysouths then moved to 102 Main Street, buying the joinery business next door.

Foundations remain in the garden for a now lost outbuilding.

Mike and Mel Day lived here in the 1990s and had the large garage and office building erected in the back garden.

65 to 67 Main Street

The 1844 enclosure map shows two houses here with outbuildings and land extending to Holme close, owned by Daniel Yarrow.

Cyril and Gwen Parson, a farming family, bought the houses now on this site around 1950. Number 67 was for his mother, Bertha, and after her death his sister-in-law. Cyril and Gwen lived here until the early 1970s.

Esther and Reg Keys were the landlord and landlady of the Plough, and after they left the pub they rented number 67.

66 Main Street (Hereward House)

There is a central Queen Anne style staircase (early 1700s) here although this might be a later imitation.

In 1916 there was a boundary dispute between the owner, George Miller, and Frederick Woodward, the landlord of the neighbouring Fox and Hounds, which gave details of previous occupants and revealing that it had been owned by the Harley family.

The first Harley recorded as living here is Jane, the widow of Thomas Harley, in 1851. There were a series of tenants until Merrington Harley, the son of Thomas and Jane move in. Merrington died in 1885 and it was inherited by his granddaughter, Elizabeth, who lived in London and rented it out. In 1887 William Jefferson lived here for four years followed by a Mr Cole and then John and Elizabeth Scarr moved here about 1893.

When Elizabeth Harley died the house was bought by George Miller of London in 1892 and he moved to live here in 1909. At some time after this, the boundary dispute was resolved as Seth Woodward bought the house.

In 1941 Grace Green of Bury House inherited Hereward House from her parents Frederick Seth and Selina Woodward, previously the landlords of the Fox and Hounds next door.

In the late 1950s and early '60s, this was the home of the headmaster of Pymoor school Mr and Mrs Mac-eke. After this Derek and Hazel Hills bought the house at auction for £600. There was no electricity and the house required a lot of renovating. There was a large garden that ran through to Eagles Lane and part of this was sold to Eddie and Kath Stearman who built a bungalow there.

The Hills sold the house to the Muskett family who subsequently sold it to Roger and Jackie Day.

68 Main Street (The Old Fox and Hounds)

The Old Fox and Hounds was built in 1723 and is an interesting mix of building materials. On the Eagles Lane end, there are some impressive lumps of masonry said to come from the Bishop's Palace and the bricks in the gable wall at the other end are smaller than modern ones. Brick sizes became larger in 1784 with the introduction of a brick tax and can be used to help date a building.

Photo Courtesy Cambridgeshire Collection

97

The modern house is two old properties that have been combined. On the corner of Eagles Lane was a bakery that was attached to the pub.

In 1881 Etches Crawley was the publican and in 1891 it was Frederick 'Seth' Woodward. Seth is described as a baker and licensed victualler and elsewhere Etches Crawley is also a baker as well as a publican. James Crawley lived in a part of the building and by 1891 was succeeded by William Crawley. In 1904 Seth was still landlord of the pub, it was owned by F. L. Harlock of Ely and had stabling for two horses and two vehicles.

In 1921 Seth Woodward sold out to Frederick Fails Taylor, who continued to run a bakery business. Frederick was described as one of the best known and most respected residents in the parish, his disposition was naturally generous and friendly to all.

Part of the building became the home of Fred and Ruth Youngs with their son, Percy, who ran a motorcycle repair business from the attached shed fronting onto Main Street. The building caught fire in 1974 and Ruth died of smoke inhalation.

Another part of the building was the home of Arthur and Elsie Green and then Violet and Jimmy Clark.

It was bought by Albert Steven, and then by Tom Mott who had the property partially restored and in 1976 extended along Eagles Lane but never lived there. It was then acquired in 1989 by the current owner Debbie Adams-Payne who completed the restoration.

69 Main Street (Railway Tavern)

This was formerly the Railway Tavern, one of two pubs in the parish to carry this name. The single-story outbuilding facing onto Main Street was a shop.

The pub was up for sale in 1851 when it was advertised as follows:

"Railway Tavern" and cottage, fronting the street, with shoemakers shop in occupation of Mr John Samson Hawkins.

Robert Hull and family, publican, in the rear garden of the Railway Tavern.

Photo Courtesy Jean Harrison

In 1861 William and Susan Kingston were the landlords followed by William and Mary Barrett. In 1883 Robert Hull married Adeline Barrett, the daughter of William and Mary and they became the landlords and were still there in 1911, Robert was a gardener and publican.

In 1904 it was owned by P. L. Hudson, Brewery, of Pampisford, Robert Hull was the landlord and it had

stabling for one horse and one vehicle.

Alver Hull, the son of Robert and Adeline emigrated to New Jersey in 1907 and worked as a painter and decorator. His return visit in 1968 made the local newspaper. Another son, Herbert, was injured when shot in the head and leg in the First War.

After closing the house became the property of the Thompson family who owned a portfolio of properties in the village. In 1955 it was sold to Henry Bye.

71 to 75 Main Street

Number 75 is the older of these three properties and they were another row of cottages owned by Grace Thompson.

The occupants of two of these houses changed on a regular basis. One of these houses, probably number 75, was the home of John and Rebecca Waddelow and family who first appear here in the 1861 census. John was a farmer of ten acres in 1871 and the family lived here until the 1900s.

Frank 'Dobbie' Gibson lived at number 71 in 1961. Frank ran the hardware store, initially next to the Nisa shop and, later, across the road next to the Club Inn.

Baptist Sunday School

Cottage replaced by the Baptist Sunday School
Photo Courtesy Cambridgeshire Collection

The Baptist schoolroom was opened in 1931, it replaced a pair of small single-story dwellings. The Baptist chapel is to the rear of the schoolroom and has a stone inscribed 'Erected A D 1788' facing onto Holme Lane. Both the chapel and schoolroom are now private homes. The chapel ceased to function in about 2010 when Chris Seekings became ill and there was no replacement to take the services.

Just below the window arch on the right-hand side, there is an engraved brick (laid sideways) that reads as follows:

Down on Joll
-ity Farm
You wanted
someone to
play with while
I wanted some
one to love
=
Dont make
my heart your
plaything
=
I'm just in
the mood
tonight
=
You were
meant for me
Izzy Azzy
Was

77 Main Street (Ferndale)

The 1900 Ordnance Survey map shows this site as undeveloped. Ferndale was built around that time by Arthur Sennitt as two cottages named after each of his daughters, Laura and Olive, the cottages were called Lauradean and Olivedean. Frank and Blanche Few bought the cottages in November 1919 and converted them into a single dwelling. The land to the rear was owned by the Few family stretching back to Cannon Street.

Peter Hampson, Frank and Blanche's grandson, and his wife Glynis have lived here since 1981.

70-74 Main Street

Photo Courtesy Cambridgeshire Collection

The row of modern houses that stretch from Eagles Lane to Acred Close replaces a row of old thatched buildings built in the early 1700s.

This row would seem to have originally consisted of a cottage on the corner of Eagles Lane, The Club Inn and the blacksmith's forge. At some point in the mid-1900s, the buildings were modified to include a shop between the cottage and the Inn.

John Simpson, a farmer of 130 acres, originally from Snettisham, was living in the cottage on the corner with his wife, Rebecca, a local girl nee Hopkin in 1851. By 1861 his acreage was reduced to 100 acres employing 4 men and 2 boys. John and Rebecca's unmarried children Philip and Rebecca remained here until sometime after 1871 when the Sabertons take over.

Next door in 1851 was Rebecca, the widow of Wright Young, with her family including her son William, a thatcher. This was presumably the Club Inn. In 1861 Denston and Charlotte Aspland had taken over before moving over the road to the Windmill.

The Saberton family first appear here in the 1871 census with William and Ann living in a property marked as the Club Inn but William's profession is given as blacksmith. William was the son of Richard and Keziah Saberton who owned the wheelwright and blacksmith business from the house behind what is now Nisa, on the opposite side of the road. There is a record from 1869 of the sale of the Club Inn, including a wheelwrights shop, outhouses, stabling, private dwelling house and fen land by George Legge. This is therefore the likely time that the Saberton Family took on this row of buildings.

Ten years later William's brother John, a wheelwright, had moved into the corner cottage before taking over his father's business, and William was now a blacksmith and publican living at the Club. Another ten years go by and William's son, Walter, is now the blacksmith living on the corner and William has died. His widow, Ann, is now the innkeeper with two of her sons, William and Joseph, working for Walter as blacksmiths assistants and this remains the situation in 1911. In 1904 the Club was owned by Wm Cutlack Brewery in Littleport and had stabling for three horses.

By 1939 Walter, now aged 83, was the publican at the Club and his son, Arthur, who people now can still remember, was the blacksmith. The blacksmith was a single-story building at the end of the row and

JUNE 1st, 1962

Fire At The Blacksmith's

WORKING in his blacksmith's shop in Main-street, Little Downham, on Tuesday morning, Mr. A. Saberton noticed something burning. He traced the source to the thatched roof of the shop, asked a neighbour to inform the Ely Fire Service and proceeded to control the outbreak with buckets of water.

The Fire Service answered the call at 10.12 a.m., and on arrival had little difficulty in extinguishing the blaze, but had to cut away a portion of the roof. This was the only daamge.

horses were sometimes shod with their back ends sticking out into the road.

Part of the Club Inn became a shop run by Frederick 'Dobbie' Gibson. This was a general hardware store and another shop that has been described as dark and a bit scary. This shop was started when the premises over the road was burnt down in 1951. Fred was joined in the business by his brother Ken after he returned from the far east having been a prisoner of war held by the Japanese.

When the pub closed it became a cottage and markings were visible on the ceiling beams where clay pipes were hung for the customers use.

In 1969 an application was approved by Ely Rural District Council Housing Committee to demolish the Club and blacksmith's workshop. The property was reportedly in a poor condition and it was owned by Peter Chambers of Holme Farm. However, in 1971 two of the cottages were still occupied and Ely County Council had refused listed building consent for demolition. It had been reported to the council that the buildings were of special architectural interest and because of their prominent position formed an important feature of the street scene. The properties were then acquired by Les Stevens and the situation was resolved in 1979 when the thatch caught fire and the buildings were destroyed.

76 -78 Main Street and Acred Close

Acred Close was the site of the Crown Joinery owned and run by Jack Acred and later taken on by his son Michael. The whole area of the site extended from Main Street to the bottom of Eagles Lane with the workshop in the middle and wood stores around the perimeter of the site.

Great memories of the house, they had a 5 hole putting green on their grass at the back.

Brian Missin had an evening job bagging up the shavings into sacks and he had a bent nail on a piece of string around his neck on which he hung the sack. That nail is now a family keepsake.

There was a house on the site occupied by Jack and then Michael and Elsie Acred. The Acreds moved to Cannon street and the house rented out until it was demolished to make way for what are now 76 and 78 Main Street. These were the last two houses to be built on the site.

Photo Courtesy Rod Waters

79 Main Street

Number 79 is a property attached to the rear of number 81 (Vine House) and was originally the servants quarters. It was bought by the Fews, a farming family who made their money hauling building material for the construction of the railway. The first recorded Fews here are John and Margaret who were living in Vine House, initially renting the whole property from the Muriel Trustees in the 1840s.

This was when the property was divided with the Fews buying the servants quarters.

In 1851 John's cousin, Elizabeth, the widow of Edward Few, a publican, is living here.

The Muriel Family

Robert Muriel was born in Suffolk in 1618 and became mayor of Cambridge in 1676. He had twelve children. The family prospered and Robert's great great grandson was Robert Muriel, a surgeon and landowner in Ely.

Robert's son, George, was baptised in Ely in 1791 and in 1803 he enrolled in the army as a cadet, serving several stints in India as an officer in the 8th Bengal Native Infantry, eventually rising to the rank of lieutenant colonel and commanding the regiment. He died of fever in 1836 at Goomsoor in Hindustan. His will leaves his estate to his son and daughter born to a native woman in India. There is a memorial to him in Ely Cathedral. George's son, George William, also rose to the rank of colonel and eventually major general and is probably the colonel Muriel referred to by the Few family. The Muriel family set up a trust to manage properties, including some in Main Street, Little Downham, one of which was rented by the Few family.

When George senior's brother, John, died in 1884 he owned 117 acres at Guildacre Farm, Little Downham.

The Few family do not appear at this property in 1861 but by 1871 John and Susan Few had moved in when John was a farmer of 60 acres, the grandson son of John and Margaret. John junior died in 1897 and Susan remained here until she died in 1907.

Robert and Susan's son, Owen Charles Few and his wife Rebecca Ann then took up residence. Number 79 was used as a farmworkers residence until extended members of the Few family once again moved in and then it was rented out until the early 2000s. It was then sold to a trust for the Duke of Northumberland, who in turn sold it to the current occupant.

81 Main Street (Vine House)

Jack Wiseman holding the horse. The children are Olive, Laura and Fred Sennitt

Number 81, Vine house, was for many years known as Sennitt's a general store and post office. The house was probably built in the late 17th century and has undergone much modification since. The building was owned by the Muriel Trustees who rented it out. It was divided into two parts, the main house and the servants quarters to the rear, in the 1840s with the Few family buying the servants quarters which is now number 79. In 1851 it was the home of Matthew and Maria Diddell. Matthew was a grocer and draper from Littleport and he was summoned for bankruptcy in 1847 but managed to remain in the house until after the 1851 census.

It was purchased by Joseph Howlett Sennitt who first appears here on the 1861 census as a grocer and draper and in 1881 also a postmaster. Joseph was the son of Edward and Alice Sennitt, a farming family from Stretham, he had 5 sons, 4 daughters and he died in 1899.

Joseph's son, Arthur, took over the business and is described in 1901 as a grocer and baker.

The baking was done by Jack Wiseman who was later the landlord of the Knife and Steel in Pymoor. The bakery was a small shed, now demolished, on the end of the row of outbuildings running between Vine House and Churchill Court.

Although the brickwork has been cleaned there is still a faint mark where the name board was.

The shop was part of the house and after Arthur's death in 1941 it became a haberdashery run by Lily Thompson.

During the war part of the house was divided for an evacuee family.

Arthur's daughters Laura and Olive were unmarried and lived here all their lives. It was still

When I biked to infant school about 70 years ago Miss Knights wouldn't allow us to leave our bikes at the school so Laura Sennitt kindly let us leave them in their little shed near the bakery.

kitted out with the counter, shelves etc. when it was sold in 1982 following the death of Laura.

Before the fire service was formed insurance companies ran their own fire services. This was in the eighteenth and nineteenth centuries. Houses would display plaques issued by the company with which they were insured. At the time of writing, Vine House

displays a plaque representing the Sun Insurance Office. Replica plaques have been made locally in recent times so this may or may not be the genuine article.

Rebecca Simpson was listed on the census as living next to the Sennitts as a shopkeeper and so may have been operating from the shop here. In 1872 she was in trouble with the law:

For the last three weeks, the Ely bench have been engaged in hearing cases from this village, under the following circumstances, the heroine being a widow named Rebecca Simpson.:- This sweet widow keeps a "sweet" shop, and on Sunday evenings some 30 or 40 young people of Little Downham patronise her by the investment of pence for lollipops, ginger-beer, cakes etc. Crowding the shop, they commence a juvenile warfare, firing at each other with ginger-beer, that is, drawing the corks, and permitting the liquid to escape in each other's faces. On leaving the scene of their exploits they attack the citadel by firing brickbats, stones and other missiles through the windows. All Downham rose in arms against these young "warlike Lords", and some of the leaders were brought before the bench. Mr Freeman, solicitor on behalf of the widow, produced a carpet bag, filled with missiles, which she alleged were picked up on the floor of her shop, thrown by the defendants, but the case was dismissed. Mr Marshall appeared for the defendants. Last Thursday, Mrs Simpson was charged with selling sweets to the boys of Downham, on Sunday, March 3rd, contrary to an act passed in the reign of a king called Charles II, and she was fined 5s and £1 17s expenses. Mr G. S. Hall appeared on her behalf, promising that she should "never do the like again".

80 to 90 Main Street and Crown Gardens

Crown Gardens is a modern development sitting on the site of the Crown Garage. The garage repaired cars, sold fuel and offered a recharging service for radio batteries which was carried out by Noble Lely.

It was started by the Murfitt family, Cyril Murfitt ran the office and George Martin the workshop.

In the 1939 Register George and Ada Martin lived here in a house to the rear of the garage with Ada's son Cyril. Ada's first Husband and Cyril's father Douglas Murfitt was described as a miller at Cyril's baptism but later started a haulage business with two lorries carrying sugar beet and was also an egg agent, a business which Ada continued.

Cyril's brother George was also involved. George Martin was listed as the proprietor, his wife, Ada, was an egg commission agent and Cyril Murfitt was an insurance agent. Later the garage was managed by Derek Green of Littleport and then John Heaps of Pymoor. Decommissioned fuel tanks are still buried deep in the back gardens there.

To the right of Crown House was a butchers shop run by Henry Lythell, described as a wooden shed, with sawdust on

Henry Lythall's exploding sausages often featured in the village panto.

the floor and meat hooks hung from the ceiling. Henry would travel around local farms slaughtering animals for personal use or to sell. In the second war, this building was used as a fire station.

There was also a fondly remembered, fish and chip shop owned by Mick Eastwood of Littleport which opened in the small office of the old garage, fronting onto Main Street, after the garage shut.

Part of the site was also used by Basil Cooper as a vegetable plot for a while and Jack Stevens ran a gents hairdressers from a small shop on this site.

There was a lane that ran down the side of the garage with a cottage at the end which was the home of Mr and Mrs Smith. Mr Smith worked as a railway crossing gatekeeper at North Fen. A Mrs Hopkin lived in a cottage behind the garage.

Churchill Court

The street frontage at Churchill Court c1920. The first house was the home of the Pate family for many years and the house with the steep roof was the Windmill pub. The telegraph pole is still in place and the square chimney stack after the Windmill is part of the village shop and is still visible.

Sisters Ethel Elizabeth and Rebecca Priscilla Pate lived in the first house in the picture which was possibly then number 85 and not reported as damaged in the fire that destroyed the neighbouring Windmill. They were the unmarried daughters of Thomas and Elizabeth Pate who were living here in 1881. Ethel was an elementary school teacher at Eagles Lane and then the school at the village hall, Rebecca did unpaid domestic duties but had been school monitor and then worked as a nursery governess for a family in Bournemouth.

Thomas Pate was the driver of a threshing engine who died age 49 in 1889 and had a non-conformist burial and on subsequent census returns Elizabeth was the owner of the threshing engine. In 1911 the family had moved to Guildacre Farm but presumably retained ownership of the house as the sisters returned to live here.

Thomas was the son of another Thomas, a farmer, and the family had lived further along Main Street at a house that had also been occupied by Thomas senior's sister Sarah Pate in 1871, age 63 and unmarried, along with Thomas' daughters, Sarah Ann and Jane, both dressmakers.

In 1904 the Windmill pub was owned by Morgan's Brewery of Norwich and had stabling for three horses and six vehicles. On the 1901 census the landlord is recorded as Warren (or Worin) Barrett but by the Ely Petty Session records of 1904 Richard Gibson is the Landlord so there was a change of licensee at this time. Previous landlords were William Lefly from Hilgay and William Williams who was described as a tailor and publican. The pub can be traced back to the early 1800s and there was a windmill nearby. These were originally owned by the Green family, descendants of whom owned the Harness makers at number 95 and also Bury House.

It would appear that Richard Gibson was the last landlord and the pub closed in the early 1900s. Richard and family were still living here in 1911.

There was a dispute involving Richard Gibson in 1919. The specific property involved is not made clear in the reporting but it may have been the old Windmill pub or possibly the building that stood where the police house is now (99 Main street).

John Stevens of the Manor House was named as the owner of the property in the dispute when he sold it to Wilfred Cole in 1919. The house was occupied by Richard Gibson who was also running a butchers shop and claimed that he had nowhere else to go. Eventually, Wilfred moved in and started up as a tobacco shop but in October 1920 the business foundered. The creditors of Wilfred Cole met at the Office of the Official Receiver and it was ascertained that the debts came to £492 7s 7d and assets amounted to £23 15s 6d. Wilfred ascribed his failure to his state of health having prevented his working regularly and five of his horses had died which was a heavy loss. The Official Receiver states that the debtor is aged 29 and was discharged from the army in 1914 as unfit. For some time he worked with his father, a farmer, and in 1917, started work as an engine driver at Norwich and then took over a smallholding in Little Downham. In march 1919 he opened a tobacco and sweet business in Little Downham.

This site was destroyed by a fire in 1951 as reported in the Ely Standard:

Considerable damage was caused by an outbreak of fire at premises in Main Street, Little Downham, on Saturday morning, two shops and living accommodation being involved.

It was at 10 a.m. that Ely Fire Formation received a call to 87 Main Street, to deal with a blazing thatched roof and on arrival they found that the fire had spread to No. 91 (now Nisa), and a second pump was summoned from Littleport. When it was obvious that the fire had gained a dangerous hold, neighbours came at once to the assistance of the unfortunate occupants with the result that most of the furniture and the stocks from the two shops (a tobacconist's and a general store) were removed to safety. Mr Saberton, however, lost a number of personal belongings.

In the first building, part of which was sub-let to Mr Frederick Gibson, tobacconist, the roof was destroyed. On the first floor the side walls collapsed and one room with its contents were severely damaged by fire and water. The remaining four rooms were damaged by water and the kitchen and the front room ceiling were also badly affected.

the extensive damage to No.91, a private house and general store occupied by Mrs Sydney Wymer, might have been prevented if the thatch had not been covered by corrugated iron sheets. These had to be stripped off in order to get at the flames, which by then had crept along and gained a firm hold. The thatch and first floor were badly damaged by fire and the ground floor, including a room sub-let to Miss Betty Martin, hairdresser, was affected mainly by water.

Overhead telephone wires were brought down by the intense heat, but Post Office engineers had a service restored later the same day. The firemen were on duty until 7 p.m.

The firemen tackled the blaze with three jets from a hydrant, but despite their efforts, both buildings were severely damaged and the occupants had to find other accommodation. The fire, first noticed by Mr Albert Saberton, the occupier of No. 87, is believed to have been caused by a chimney spark blown onto the thatch. The roof covering the whole of the involved premises was destroyed, but the fire was confined to the upper part of the buildings the chief damage downstairs being caused by water.

The tobacconist business was run by Frederick 'Dobbie' Gibson, the son of Richard the butcher, who moved to a shop over the road after the fire.

The site remained derelict for several years and in 1968 became the site for Churchill Court. This was not without controversy again reported in the local paper.

The corrugated fence at Churchill Court, Little Downham, which has annoyed residents by rattling in the wind and even keeping awake at night a deaf lady, is to be replaced by a close boarded fence.

When complaints about the fence were aired at the annual parish meeting and reported in this paper. Miss Alice Minnie Scott said that, though deaf, she was troubled at night by the wind rattling the fence which is a flat away from her home.

Reporting at last Wednesday's meeting of the Ely Rural District Housing Committee the architect, Mr N Russell, said that maintenance work on the recently built site had yet to be completed and though notice had been given to the contractors, Law Bros (Builders) Ltd., the work had not been done.

He was authorised to give final warning to the contractors and if the work had not been completed after 28 days, to hand over to another contractor.

Coun. R W Parson, chairman of Little Downham Parish Council, asked what action had been taken over the fence.

Mr Russell replied that in the original contract the fence was to be replaced with a brick wall. Now the work was being put out to a different contractor and the aim was to replace it with a close-boarded fence.

There was a bakery on the site called the Windmill Bakery. The first census entry for this business was in 1911 when Herbert Gregory, a baker from Rutland, was living here behind the Windmill pub. In 1939 Alf Saberton was running a bakery on this site and is listed here with his wife Christine. Alf was the son of Walter who worked at the blacksmith forge on the opposite side of the road.

Village Shop

In 1871 Denston and Charlotte Aspland are living next door at the Windmill Pub with Denston described as a surveyor and collector (presumably of taxes) and the shop is occupied by James Savage, grocer from Hilgay, who is unmarried. In 1881 the shop is unoccupied and Charlotte Aspland took on the shop at some time in the 1880s after her husband, Denston died in 1882. Charlotte's son William succeeded her as a grocer here.

In 1911 Annie Royal was living here as a shopkeeper with two boarders: Sarah Cox an assistant in household duties and shop work and Harold Seal, Carpenter and Wheelwright. Presumably, Harold was working for John Saberton running the wheelwrights from the house behind the shop. Annie was married to Joseph Royal from Pimlico who was a sawyer and died in 1909. On the 1939 register Annie Lofts, retired shopkeeper, was living here and she was at one time running the business until Lewis Hull takes over the shop.

In 1951 the fire in the neighbouring cottage damaged this property too when it comprised of a private house and general store occupied by Ivy Wymer with a room sub-let to hairdresser Betty Martin.

Ivy was married to Sydney, an electrician with a false hand as the result of an accident. As well as a general store they also sold radios and electrical goods.

The Wymers were succeeded by John and June Murfitt. In 1967 the Murfitt family sold it on to Ivy Proctor.

> One of my sons bought a tennis ball from Proctor's and it didn't bounce. When he took it back and asked to change it Mrs Proctor said it was the non bouncing sort.

The shop was bought in the 1990s by a family who also bought number 50 and combined the businesses into these premises. They subsequently sold the shop to the current owners, Kenny and Harpal Atwal. It has been variously branded as Costcutters and Nisa.

- December 7th/8th, 1967

£3,025 FOR DOWNHAM STORE

A general stores and dwelling house changed hands for £3,025 at a sale held in the Newnham-street clubroom, Ely, on Thursday.

The price was paid by Mrs. I Proctor of Main-street, Witchford, for numbers 91 and 91a Main-street, Little Downham, offered for sale by direction of Mrs. E. Murfitt.

The auctioneers were A T Grain and Sons of Ely and the vendors' solicitors were Messrs. Archer and Archer.

The property comprised, on the ground floor, a living room, pantry, kitchen, lounge and two shops.

First floor comprised of three bedrooms and bathroom.

92 Main Street (Crown House)

Crown House was formerly the Crown Pub and there has also been a bakery on the site.

The earliest identifiable publican here from the census returns is James Strawson in 1871 with his wife, Charlotte, son and daughter and six boarders and lodgers. The property is unoccupied in 1881 but by 1891 David and Elizabeth Eley were the publicans. David was born in Ely but Elizabeth was from Yorkshire and their children were born in Rochdale, Nottingham and Little Downham. By 1901 David was a horse keeper back in Rochdale with the family.

On the 1901 census, the property is again shown as unoccupied but by the 1904 Ely Petty Session records the landlord was John Leaford, it was owned by A&B Hall of Ely

The old bakery to the rear of the Crown pub.
Photo Courtesy Zoie James

and had stabling for one horse and one vehicle. John died in 1906 and Caroline remained living here with four lodgers and a servant.

George Pinckard "Gubby" Taylor
Photo Courtesy Alan Martin

118

The Taylor family were bakers who bought both the Fox and Hounds and, in 1921, the Crown. Head of the family Frederick Taylor bought the Fox and Hounds and the deeds show that the Crown was transferred to his wife Emily. Their son George Pinckard Taylor was a master baker and ran the business here. George served in World War 1 and was discharged on medical grounds in 1917. He was described as being of a most cheerful disposition and being best remembered for his regular delivery service over a period of 50 years. George died in 1961.

The house has been renovated by Zoie James and family.

93 Main Street

93 Main Street 1970
Photo Courtesy Rod Waters

There is a new house behind the village shop that replaces an older building which had a long narrow front garden leading down to a small cottage.

For many years this was the home of the Saberton family. Richard Saberton was born in Ely in 1806 the son of John Saberton, labourer, and Mary. He married Keziah Waddelow in 1827 and is first recorded as a blacksmith here in 1841. Richard died in 1864 and Keziah remained living here until she died in 1887. There were Sabertons in Little Downham in the 1600s but then a gap in the 18th century, after which the current branch of the Sabertons arrived in the parish and the Saberton Families now in Little Downham can be traced back to Richard and Keziah.

John Saberton the son of Richard and Keziah married Abigail Moxon in 1870 and took on the business when Richard died, although he was living across the road until his mother died after which he moved in here. Abigail was the daughter of William Moxon, another blacksmith in Main Street. They had sons, Elisha who was a carpenter, Moxon, a wheelwright and Elias, a blacksmith.

In 1951 Mary and Ada Saberton lived here, Mary died in 1956 and Ada remained here until she died in 1974. Mary and Ada were the daughters of John and Abigail Saberton.

Lost Buildings

Photo Courtesy Cambridgeshire Collection

The 1925 Ordnance Survey map shows a series of buildings between The Club Inn and Crown pub, all now lost. Some of them were demolished on the site that became the Crown Garage and some were associated with Acred's Yard. These in turn have disappeared to make way for modern housing. There are many more entries in the census returns than can be accounted for by the current housing footprint and these must have referred to residents of these now lost buildings.

One of the buildings here was a smithy and associated residence, approximately opposite number 101. The last recorded blacksmith was William Moxon who was living here with his wife Elizabeth, and brother Samuel, in 1911. In 1891 William's father William Moxon senior was the blacksmith here with his sons Richard, a blacksmith, Reuben, a wheelwright and Samuel, also a wheelwright. William senior is the first recorded blacksmith at this site.

William senior was the son of Matthew Moxon who served an apprenticeship with Robert Harris in 1808 as a shoemaker but spent most of his working life as an agricultural labourer.

Between the Club Inn and Crown garage was a house called "The Long House". This was the home of Rebecca Few in 1939, who had previously lived at 79 Main Street and was sold, in 1945 when Rebecca died, to the Acreds. It was described as a substantial residence with outbuildings, garage and two acres of grazing paddock. Although water was laid on it had a spring well in the garden. The attached farm had a loosebox, thatched granary and barn both fronting Main Street and also a cattle shed.

Chambers Way (Chambers Yard)

W. B. Chambers and Sons was a vegetable merchant and also a coal merchant. The farmyard was converted into business premises in the 1940s. To the left of the entrance was Holme House and to the right were the offices with the yard and sheds behind, a large potato shed just behind the house and a packing shed at the bottom of the yard. Lorry drivers from both the UK and Europe would turn up with deliveries at all hours. The business also had a seasonal depot in Pembrokeshire dealing with early potatoes. Les Stevens was the office manager here before buying the Bishop's Palace and associated farm.

W. B. Chambers farm workers

94 Main Street (Holme House)

This was the home of the Chambers family who owned the business that operated in Chambers Yard. In 1901 and 1911 it was the home of James and Elizabeth

I remember it with a white metal fence. We had a beautifully scented plant on the small wall in the garden to the left and a pear tree up the house wall on the right.

Chambers and eight children. The last of that family who lived here were James' son Bert and his wife May Chambers. Bert Chambers was actually Waddelow Bertram Chambers and, although the Chambers were a local family, he was born in Wigan whilst his father was working there as a grocer and milk purveyor.

James married Elizabeth Chambers in 1887 and was the son of another couple called James and Elizabeth Chambers. At the age of

22, James junior was a carpenter like his father. Before James, this was the home of Elijah Chambers, a farmer from Coveney, with his wife Rebecca and several generations of extended family. It is unclear whether James was related to Elijah.

When Bert and May moved out it became the home of the family of Frank Judd who was the company Secretary for W. B. Chambers.

The original railings were removed during the second war as part of the campaign to collect metal for the war effort.

The Bennett family moved here in 2009 and then it was sold to the Morton family who carried out substantial modifications.

LITTLE DOWNHAM'S LATEST !

Freak Egg This Time.

Turning the scale at seven ounces, an egg has been laid by a hen belonging to Mr .W. B. Chambers, of Holme Farm, Little Downham.

When broken open, another full-sized egg, complete with shell, was found inside. The white of the outside egg was roughly three times larger than the ordinary size, but the yolk was unusually small.

95 Main Street

Woods Green was born in Downham Market in 1773, the son of William and Ann Green. There were already several Green families in Little Downham at that time, including Christopher Green, a publican, who died age 62 in 1803 and who seems to have been a precursor to the later line of publicans in the Green family. Woods Green was apprenticed as a miller to Christopher Green of Little Downham in 1792 and married Ann Baddely of Woburn in Bedfordshire in 1793. Woods and Ann had six children, including William Baddely Green who became a miller, Christopher, a publican and Thomas a victualler. The family prospered and Woods became a farmer owning land, a pub and a windmill. In the early

1820s, Woods sold up and moved to Bedfordshire but his children remained in Little Downham.

Photo Courtesy Alan Martin

Woods' son Christopher was the landlord of the Windmill pub, he marries Sophia Waddelow and they had a son, William.

Today some people can remember this as a harness maker and cycle shop. There are no leather workers here on the 1861 census but there is an unoccupied property and in 1851 Samuel Robson a Saddler and general dealer from Aylsham in Norfolk was living here or nearby. A sales notice dated 9th May 1856 showed that the highest bidder at auction was a Samuel Robson and he paid eighty-six pounds, therefore he must have bought the property after renting it for some time. In 1861 William Green was living with his brother, Robert, a butcher, elsewhere in Main Street and gave his profession as harness maker. On William's marriage to Hannah Coplin in 1868, he again gives his profession as harness maker and by 1871 William and Hannah are living here.

When William and Ann have a son in 1871 they name him William after his father and Woods for his grandfather. William Woods Green is living in Litcham, Norfolk in 1891 and is following in the family occupation of saddler.

William senior dies in 1895, and William Woods takes over the business, puts his name over the door and is head of the household here in 1901 with his family and brother Charles, also a saddler. By 1911 William Woods is a farmer, first at Tower Farm and later Bury Farm, Charles is living here and presumably running the business.

Fred Green could make anything in leather – saddles, harness, whips etc. The smell in his workshop was wonderful.

By the time of the 1939, register Charles Green's son Alfred was here, listed as a cycle agent and harness maker and had a bicycle shop. Alfred was the last Green to have a business here and it became a private residence but the signs of the original shop are still evident in the brickwork.

Between this shop and the neighbouring village store, there was a wooden structure built across what is now a drive between the two buildings. This was a storeroom for the Greens.

96 Main Street (Holly Tree Cottage)

This is a modern house that stands on the site of a small old cottage. In 1939 George and Elizabeth Barber lived here. The best-remembered resident is Lewis Hopkin who ran a barbers from the premises. It seems that he had one style based on a set of bowler hats hanging on one wall of the cottage, they would be fitted onto the customers head and formed a template for the haircut. If the light inside wasn't good enough customers would get their hair cut on the pavement in the street. Lewis was the son of William and Kate Hopkin who lived in Cannon Street and the family were Freemasons.

The house was demolished and the land used as a rose garden by Vera Buttress of the neighbouring property until the present house was built.

97 Main Street (The Trees)

A lovely old thatched house The Trees is hidden behind a large hedge, a grade II listed building built in the 15th century. It is a late medieval hall house with original roof timbers blackened from the fires that would have heated it

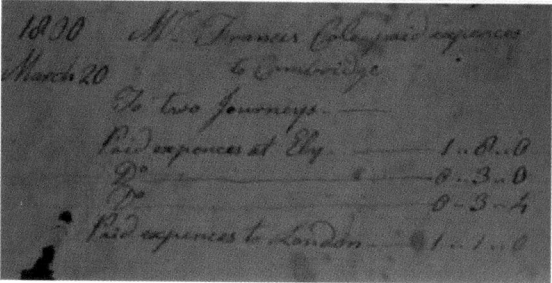

A receipt to Francis Cole dated 1800
Courtesy Mike England

as an open hall. It is a timber-framed building which has associations with the Bishop's Palace and has been updated over time including the addition of a floor to create an upper storey. The remains of a large medieval barn are in the garden

It has been home to the Cole family for many generations and their fortunes can be traced through the census returns.

Restored inglenook fireplace
Photo Courtesy Mike England

126

A receipt found during restoration shows that Francis Cole was living here in 1800 and had been reimbursed for travel to Cambridge. By 1851 a younger Francis Cole and his wife Mary lived here with seven children farming 100 acres and, ten years later, this had grown to 150 acres, with three sons working on the farm as labourers and his daughter Sarah Ann as a dairymaid.

In 1841 and 1851 Francis' neighbour was his father John, but it is unclear whether this was a separate property or, more likely, number 97 was divided into more than one household.

By 1871 the farming enterprise was reduced to 70 acres but still employing three men and ten years later it was reduced further to 62 acres and one man, although they could still employ Ellen Scarrow as a servant. Francis died in 1899 aged 97. Francis' son Flanders dug a hole in the floor so that his grandfather clock could stand up in the room. Flanders predeceased his father and when his wife Mary died in 1903 their son, Francis, inherited the property. Francis junior was a railway clerk and he died in 1940.

The house remained in the Cole family until 1967 or '68 when it was bought by David Ranson who had it re-thatched by Fred and Herbert Oldfield of Whittlesey. It is currently the home of the England family.

The first Cole recorded in the parish registers is Ellen Cole who married John Blench in 1587 and the Coles of 97 Main Street can probably be traced back to this Cole family.

98 Main Street (Ida Grove Cottage)

This house was built in 1916 by the Harrison family and lived in by Alfred, Sarah (nee Brittain) and their children, Vernon and Vera Maria. The 1900 Ordnance survey map shows a building with a similar footprint but set further back from the road. The 1901 and 1911 census names John Brittain smallholder and father of Sarah Brittain as living here and this was presumably demolished to make

> *I remember Mrs Buttress. When living at the Plough my mum would get wool from her, it was a cute little shop. I remember she had a life size baby doll in the window dressed in baby clothes that had been knitted. I as a little girl loved that doll and dreamt that one day I could have one just like that. I don't know if Mrs Buttress was moving or just heard how much I loved that doll but one Christmas I opened my present and it was my beloved doll, she had given it to my mum for me. It was the best Christmas ever. My heart is full every time I think of her.*

way for the current house. John Brittain was also a thatcher, son of Samuel, a thatcher.

The Harrisons were farmers, Vera married Roland Buttress in 1939 and they moved to Littleport. Later Vera moved back to Ida Grove, probably after the death of her parents, and lived here until her death in 1987. She ran a shop from the front room, selling general household items including wool, and material.

It is thought that the name of the cottage is in recognition of a relative that went to Iowa, America and sent money back to help fund the building of the new property. There were a few people called Ida Grove living in Iowa at this time and there is also a town called Ida Grove.

99 (The Old Police House)

Here was the home of the village policeman with a small single-storey room at the front which served as the police station. The architect's plans are dated November 1964 and so the house must have been built shortly after this by Maurice Jordan, a well known local builder.

In 1877 a list of candidates to be parish constables for a number of parishes around Ely was presented to the Petty Sessions meeting. The parish constable from Oxlode and Downham attended the meeting and said that he would refuse to serve unless he was provided with a staff and handcuffs. There was a debate as to whether the county or parish should bear the cost for this and it was eventually decided that it was the responsibility of the parish.

Before the police house, there was a butcher's shop on this site.

The 1844 enclosure map marks this land as belonging to John Thomas Waddington who was baptised at Ely cathedral in 1796 and was the son of Thomas Waddington, Rector of St Leonard's.

The first recorded butcher at this address is Edward Langford from Stretham in 1851 and by 1861 Christopher Green had taken over the business. He was still there in 1881, but ten years later his son Edmund was the head of the household with his wife, Caroline, and children, Percy and Myrtle. Christopher was the grandson of Woods Green and it is therefore, the same family who were saddlers and harness makers nearby. Edmund was the last butcher recorded in the census here but the shop was still in existence when it was for sale in 1922. Richard Gibson, landlord of the nearby Windmill pub was a publican and butcher so it is possible that he was living at the pub and running a butcher's business from here.

For a brief period, it is remembered as a harness maker's run by a Mr Newell.

DOWNHAM, ISLE OF ELY.

SALE OF A VALUABLE

FREEHOLD PROPERTY

With Vacant Possession at Michaelmas next,

COMPRISING

A Dwelling House, Butcher's Shop,

REGISTERED SLAUGHTER HOUSE,

STABLE, OUTBUILDINGS,

AND

LARGE GARDEN,

Situate in the Main Street, in the Village of Downham,

WHICH

GEORGE COMINS

Is favoured with instructions from the Owner, to Offer for Sale by Auction

AT THE BELL HOTEL, ELY,

On THURSDAY, 7th SEPTEMBER, 1922,

At FOUR o'clock in the Afternoon, precisely,

Subject to such Conditions of Sale as will be then produced.

PARTICULARS.

A Brick-built and Thatched DWELLING HOUSE, containing on the Ground Floor—Living Room with Cupboard and Stove, large Kitchen with Cooking Stove, Oven and Cupboard. On the First Floor—3 Bed Rooms.

A Brick-built and Tiled BUTCHER'S SHOP fitted with Counter, Shelves, Rails and Hooks.

The BUILDINGS comprise—A Brick-built and Thatched Registered SLAUGHTER HOUSE with Concrete Floor, and New Copper and Furnace.

A Brick-built and Tiled WASH HOUSE with Copper and Furnace, Open Hearth and Brick Oven; a similar Built STORE PLACE, a Brick, Timber-built and Boarded Loose Box; a similar Built Pigsty; a new Timber-built and Boarded Earth Closet with Tiled Roof, and an Iron Pump with a good supply of Water, and

A LARGE GARDEN.

This Property has a Frontage of about 40 feet 8 inches to the Main Street, and a Depth of 141 feet, or thereabout, and contains an Area of

610 SQUARE YARDS

(more or less).

Bounded North by the Main Street; South by Property of Mr. John H. Stevens; East by Property of Mr. Frank Cole; and West by Properties of Mr. John H. Stevens, Mr. J. Leaford, and Messrs. A. and B. Hall.

Land Tax believed to be exempt.

Particulars of Sale may be obtained of Messrs. HALL & CAMPBELL, Solicitors, Ely, or of GEORGE COMINS, Auctioneer, Valuer, and Land Agent, Ely.

J. H. CLEMENTS AND SON, PRINTERS, ELY.

The Apple Lodge

The Apple Lodge was used to store apples when the garden was an orchard. It was converted in the 1990s.

100 Main Street (Bramley House)

The 1900 ordnance survey map shows this to be open space. The house was built for William (Ginger) Moxon, a fruit and asparagus grower, and his wife Ellen, around 1910 and they lived there until their daughter Ada married Arthur Chambers. Ginger moved into an extension on the Chapel side of the house known as Granddad's kitchen. When Arthur and Ada

> *We used to spend hours in the orchard behind his house bird nesting and with air rifles – happy days.*

died in the 1950s their son Cliff lived in the house until the 1980s. The Runciman family moved here in the 1990s.

101 Main Street (The Old Red, White and Blue)

The Red White and Blue was popular with the local farmers and was a darts pub, there was always a long waiting list to get on the dartboard.

> *I remember going in for some tobacco for my father. It was taken out of a storage tin, weighed and rolled up in a white twist of paper with Brunnings printed on it in blue writing.*

James Leaford was the publican here in 1861 and 1871. In 1881 Philip Thompson was head of the household with his wife Maria and their eleven children.

*Photo Courtesy
Cambridgeshire Collection*

In 1904 it was owned by A&B Hall of Ely. and had stabling for five horses, the landlord was William Moxon and by 1911 Page Cole is living here. Philip Thompson was the only resident described as publican. James Leaford, William Moxon and Page Cole were all labourers so publican may have been a secondary income for the landlords.

Mr and Mr Evans ran it in the 1950s. Percy 'Tid' Nicholas and his wife, Bella, were here from 1964 until 1968 after which it was converted into a house. During restoration in 2012, a flint was found in the chimney inscribed "John South 1857"

The current deeds state that the owners are prohibited from selling wine, beer, spirits etc.

If you look at the right hand side window ledge at the Red, White and Blue you will see that it is worn. This is where in the 1930s the young lads of the village used to sharpen their pen knives. They used that spot because, at night, there was a gap in the curtains and that spot was always illuminated.

When number 99 was sold as a butchers shop in 1922 Mr J Leaford still owned land adjacent to this site.

101A Main Street

This is an old barn which was part of the estate of the neighbouring Manor House and the plaque on the side suggests that it was built in 1772. The 1884 enclosure map shows a range of buildings extending behind the barn to Cross Lane. Peter Chambers bought the farm and renovated the barn which was used as a store shed then converted to a cold store for vegetables. It was later sold for conversion.

103 Main Street (Manor House)

The Lord of the Manor of Downham is the Bishop of Ely and in the 1800s much of the land associated with this farmhouse was held by William Martin on lease from the Bishop of Ely who may also have owned this house, or the house may have been associated with the bishop's Manor Farm which would explain the name.

On the early census, this is the home of William Martin age 50 where he is a farmer of 630 acres with 29 labourers. William died in 1853 and was replaced by his nephew, also William, son of Henry Martin, Gentleman. William junior was married to Ann Cooke who was born in Loughborough and their children were born in Fordham, Norfolk. William junior is farming 600 acres employing 34 men, 10 girls and 10 boys and later moved to Ely where he died in 1882.

The Martins were succeeded at the Manor House by William and Caroline Johnson from the Norfolk-Lincolnshire border, their ten children and understandably, Sarah Berryman, nursemaid. By this time the farm holding associated with the house had fallen to 400 acres. On the 1886 Ordnance Survey map, there is a large ornamental garden shown beside the house.

The house was derelict. Kids of the village would sometimes trespass into it, we thought it was haunted. There was a dilapidated piano in one room. The basement was flooded.

The 1891 census suggests that John Rix, Farm Bailiff, may have lived here. Occupation of the house after this changed regularly until it became the farmhouse for J. H. Stevens and Son owned by John Henry Stevens who died in 1936, the son was Tom. In the 1950s John Stevens and his wife Josy lived in the Manor House, John mostly kept pigs and cattle in the yard. Manor House was bought by Peter

Chambers from John Stevens when it still had a farmyard. Peter Chambers lived in the house and used the yard as lorry depot. The house has been renovated by various owners since John Stevens to become the building that it is today.

105A Main Street

105A is a new house built on land formerly part of the grounds of the Manor House.

105 - 115 Main Street (The Barracks)

The six semi-detached houses that lead to the corner of Main Street and Townsend sit on the site of a group of houses known as the Barracks which stretched back to Cross Lane.

In 1911 nine dwellings are occupied by farm labourers between Bramley House and the end of the Barracks. These are probably the row of dwellings that front the Barracks onto Main Street. There are no other buildings shown on the 1900 Ordnance Survey map.

Villages often had a group of cottages clustered around a yard and known as the barracks, though without any military link.

The Barracks were demolished in the 1930s and replaced by the current houses.

Community Rooms

The Methodists of Little Downham first met in a barn in Cannon Street and then moved to premises at Townsend before acquiring the land to build this chapel. They purchased the site from John Russell who in turn had bought it in 1842 from William Tingey.

Built in 1877, this was the chapel until a larger chapel was built next door and it became the Sunday school. Following the integration of the local Methodist and Anglican communities, it is now used as the church hall and community rooms.

Methodist Chapel

The old chapel has the inscription 'Weslyan Church' above the front window and '1907' over the front door. This was the date that the foundation stone was laid and it was opened at Easter 1908. It was built by a Mr King of Exning at a cost of £579 3s 0d.

It was a typical Methodist chapel of its time, going in through the front door, and then right or left to the entry doors and there was no middle aisle. Coffins had to be slid through a hatch onto the pews as the turn was too tight to go through the front and then side doors. Emma Hull used to play the organ in the chapel for all the services every Sunday, and never missed a day until she died in the mid-1950s. For many years in the 1970s and '80s, John and June Murfitt ran the chapel. The chapel was sold and converted in 2002 and is now a private house.

102 Main Street

The Rayners are first recorded here in 1851 with John Rayner, wheelwright, although the family are recorded in the parish records in the 1600s. When John Rayner married Maria Hall in 1823 he was a labourer, Maria was a straw bonnet maker and their son Henry was a wheelwright, although he was blind. When the Bysouth family moved into the house they

Photo Courtesy David Bysouth

found some equipment for enabling a blind person to read music which may well have belonged to Henry. John's sister-in-law, Sarah, was widowed shortly after marriage and earned her living as a publican both at the George and Dragon and the Plough. John died in 1864, Maria and Henry remained in the house with another son, Philip, living over the road as a wheelwright and blacksmith, probably in what is now number 6 Townsend, Blacksmith's Cottage. Ten years later Philip had added an extra income being described as wheelwright, blacksmith and grocer. By 1891 Philip and his family had moved into number 102 along with Maria and Henry. Maria died in 1892 aged 85 and Henry in 1901, leaving Philip and family as the occupants with Philip's son, John becoming employed as a carpenter.

The house currently on the site, in the form shown in the photo, was built around 1894 and so must have replaced an earlier building that was the original Rayner home. It is possible that Philip had the new house built after his mother died.

Philip and Eunice Bysouth and family moved to Little Downham from

> My dad's first job when leaving school was working for Bysouth's making coffins.

Knebworth in 1935 and lived in Alpha Cottage (64 Main Street) until Philip bought the business and house from the Rayners. Philip's son David remembers moving into the house and that the doors and windows were all second-hand and of different designs, modified to fit the new house. He also remembers that part of the house had once been used as a shop, possibly a milliner's, following Maria Rayner's profession.

This is now a much larger house than the original in this picture. Cyril and Gwen Murfitt lived here in the 1950s with their children Phillipa and Joanne and they had it extended.

Ambrose's Workshop

A cart and wagon makers business here had been run by the Raynor family since the early 1700s and it was then bought by Philip Bysouth. It became known as Ambrose's when it was taken

> We used to go to the workshop on the way home from school to get sawdust for our rabbits.

Photo Courtesy John Clarke

over again in the 1950s. A modern house now stands where the joinery workshop once was but there are some original walls remaining with markings thought to be for measuring coffin sizes. Two people who worked there were Hubert Roe who lived in Tower Road and who was also the head man at the Baptist Church and Sooty Evans, who was the landlord of The Rifleman's Arms in Lynn Road, Ely. Frank Saberton was employed by the Bysouths as a blacksmith until he took over his father's smithy, opposite the village hall. They also operated as undertakers and one memory is of the coffins that they made and that they used to have a hearse and a bier in the workshop. Several people remember collecting sawdust from the joinery for their pets.

The Plough

Stories about the Plough could fill a book on their own, here are just a few. In 1904 Ann Hopkin of West Mount (a house on the other side of the green at Townsend) was the owner and leased it to Greene King. John Cooper was the landlord although the 1901 census names Edgar Leeks, shepherd, as living there with John Cooper living over the road in Townsend with his grandmother, Ann Hopkin, and also working as a miller. By 1911 John Cooper was still landlord and now living on the premises. He is described as labourer and potato merchant which reflects an era when running a pub wasn't a living on its own and was a second job. Johnny Walker, known as Pops, was a well-remembered landlord in the 1940s and '50s. Men came to sit in the taproom to chat and warm up their beer from a poker heated in the fireplace, they played darts and pitch penny and there was a piano in the other room. Most of the regulars drank mild, which was the most popular choice, some had brown and mild and some preferred Guinness. There was a sweeter beer called Harvest Brown which was bottled.

As you came into the front door, to the left was the taproom with wooden benches on either side, to the right was the piano and club room. At the back, the

> I remember playing so many games of pitch penny, it was so much fun. Lots if betting among the locals. Dominoes was played too.

underground cellar was on the right where the beer was in barrels, a dark cold old room. A room which was above the cellar was used as a bedroom. On the left was the living room and the kitchen beyond that with three further rooms upstairs. Outside were two sheds, one was the greyhounds home and other a coal shed. The ladies toilets were to the right consisting of wooden home made squares of wood with a hole in the centre, one for grown-ups and one for a child. They were like a shed with a door and the men's were opposite and known as 'the trough'.

One Landlord, Reg Keys, was often in the local news for unusual charity stunts.

In 1975 Reg and Esther Keys handed the pub on to Another well-regarded landlord, George Adams and his wife June. There was a comment about the Plough in the 'Good Pubs Guide' as 'a pleasant but unexceptional pub made special by the character of its landlord, Mr George Adams.' When they took it on it was half the size that it is now, it ended where the wooden step is inside the pub. One of the provisos was that they had to extend it and bring the toilets inside. The bottom bar needed furniture and June drove all the way to London in a VW and brought the chairs and tables home. Maurice Jordan did the building work and Richard Ambrose was the architect. The old plough that stands outside was bought by George Adams.

The pub is currently run by Peter, Wasana and Wut Allen and is well known for its authentic Thai food.

The Pound

Photo Courtesy Cambridgeshire Collection

Many villages had a pound, it was for stray animals whose owners had to pay to retrieve them. The Little Downham pound was owned by the Parish Council but by the end of the 19th century had fallen out of use. There were proposals by the Parish Council to demolish it but fortunately, this was not followed through and it was eventually sold to an electricity company for use as a substation. Some people remember it as pit pound because it was used as a rubbish dump. In 2002 the Parish Council made an enquiry about the possibility of reacquiring the pound and restoring it as a local amenity. The electricity company would only agree if the council met the cost of moving the substation which was beyond the council's means. In the early 1900s, the Main street was lit by gas lamps and these were supplied by a small gasworks in the corner of the pound.

Martin's Lane

The top of Martin's Lane is the highest point in Little Downham at 21 metres (69 feet) above sea level. Old maps show a range of buildings behind the barn that is now 101 Main Street which was part of Manor Farm and owned in 1844 by William Martin and this family is presumably the origin of this road's name. There were also some buildings opposite the end of Cross Lane. Martin's Lane rarely features on census returns but in 1861 There were three households;

Elizabeth Barrett, a tailoress; Isabella Denston, a dressmaker and Elizabeth Meadows.

Barn on the corner of Martin's Lane and Cross Lane
Photo Courtesy Cambridgeshire Collection

On the census for other years these women are listed as living in Main Street. In 1891 Rebecca Gilbert was living here.

Nature Reserve

The land for the first acquired part of the nature reserve was owned by Johnny Miles, it had not been intensively farmed and was considered suitable for conservation. Reg Gilbert owned the land before Johnny Miles. He had a large copper there for boiling potatoes to feed pigs.

The parish council had the foresight to buy two fields in 1997 by launching a public subscription campaign. This prompted the formation of the Conservation Volunteers to establish and manage the nature reserve that resulted from the purchase. Derick and Helen Last were the guiding lights in forming the Conservation Volunteers and Derick became the first chairman, succeeded by Keith Norton.

Of the original two fields, the northern one was planted up with native trees to become Pingle Wood. The planting was a community event held on 29th November 1997. The cart shed was built later as part of the millennium celebrations to become a home for old agricultural implements donated by local farmers and to house information boards. It is built on the site of old pigsties that were made from reclaimed bog oak. It is said that the entrance next to the cart shed was improved by burying old gravestones to harden the roadway. Pingle wood has been used for several subsequent projects including a wild flower patch and bee hives. The field to the south of Pingle Wood is called Miles Meadow and is used for traditional cattle grazing. I am told that many years ago there was an outbreak of anthrax and that the affected animals are buried in Miles Meadow.

The nature reserve was expanded with the addition of the Holts in 2000 to include traditional sheep grazing. Of the five fields that make up this area, three were purchased from Den Harrison of Lawns Farm and Den bequeathed the other two. There is an overgrown area to the north of the main field which was once a cottage with a garden and the remnants of an orchard can be found among the trees.

Another addition to the Nature Reserve was the Community Orchard which was planted on 17th December 2005 on land owned by the County Council rented on a sixty-year lease. It was originally planted with sixteen varieties of old Cambridgeshire apples, four of each, and has been added to over the subsequent years.

Pond Lane

On maps as far back as 1866 this is marked as Pond Lane but locally, and on census returns, it was known as Pit Lane. The name gradually changed through Pit/Pond Lane to Pond Lane. The census shows that between 1841 and1911 there were three households in Pond Lane inhabited by agricultural workers. In 1850 a house was advertised for sale: A Brick built and thatched cottage, turf lodge and garden containing 16 perches, situate in Pit Lane, and in the occupation of George South. It was advertised again in 1858, this time occupied by George's son William. The thatched cottage in the photograph was the home of Isaac and Daisy Moxon and later their son Basil, a popular Little Downham resident.

Photo Courtesy Alan Martin

Two other houses in the photo were originally Feoffees properties but they were put up for sale in 1893, described as brick-built cottages in the occupation of John Lofts and William Cornwell, reserve price £50. The Feoffees still retained a house in Pond lane and in 1921 the treasurer asked for authority to fix a copper into the house in Pit Lane as no accommodation for boiling washing was available. It was granted. By 1963 the house was derelict and was advertised to be let as a store and in 1967 it was decided to sell the property.

The pond was used for public baptism, one of which was reported in the local paper:

18 September 1910 – A particular extraordinary affair occurred at Little Downham on Sunday

afternoon last. There was a public baptismal service in the village and some hundreds of persons had assembled round the village pond situate in Cannon Street to witness what is in this district an uncommon and novel ceremony.

Little knowledge had any spectator of the disgraceful scene which was to follow and interrupt the proceedings.

The crowd waited patiently fully anticipating to witness something rare. The Rev Edward Morris of London, wading into the water which is invariably used for watering horses and suchlike, made preparations for the immersion.

Following close upon the minister was the wife of a well known inhabitant of the village. She was prepared for the ceremony and was about to be immersed when a voice known to all shouted words of objection. Looking in the direction of the interrupter the crowd beheld the husband of the woman in a very agitated condition.

His very presence was evidence of protests and having regard to his wishes, the ceremony so far as the woman was concerned, should have been postponed immediately, but the minister and the wife paid little heed to her husband's objection and the ceremony was proceeded with.

The man, who was separated from the rest of the assembly by a hedge, immediately scaled a wooden fence some distance away and hurried to the pond. Further agitation prevailed when he arrived on the scene. The minster had immersed his wife in the centre of the pond and the ceremony was over.

The man thereupon waded into the water protesting most vehemently, the whole time the crowd was speculating as to what would happen next, when the husband, followed by his brother and the local policeman, left the scene. However, he met his wife immediately afterwards and reproached her severely for so acting against his wishes.

The Rev E Morris continued the service and a male candidate was immersed without further disturbance. The occurrence altogether has caused considerable stir amongst the villagers of Little Downham

The couple involved were Robert and Adeline Hull. Robert was the landlord of the Railway Tavern on Main Street and didn't believe in religion whereas Adeline was a regular chapel goer.

The pond fell out of use and became considered a health hazard. It was filled in during the 1940s.

Sheep at the pond with Reg Gilbert
Photo Courtesy Alan Martin

School Lane

This was a private road serving land owned by the Feoffees and had a gate which was closed for one day a year in order to prevent it becoming a public right of way. The Feoffees accounts for the 1760s refer to land rented to the Reverent Thomas Jones in Town House Close. This refers to the Feoffees original name of the Town Houses and Lands charity and is probably the original name for this lane. The 1844 enclosure map shows that the land on the west side was owned by Daniel Jones, probably a descendant of Thomas. The Feoffees records have many references to gardens (allotments) and orchards in School Lane with much discussion about using the orchard behind the school to extend its buildings.

The first recorded name on maps and in the census returns for this road was Workhouse Lane and changed to School Lane to reflect the change of use of the building that is now the Village Hall on the corner. On the 1901 census, it is called School Lane but on the subsequent 1911 census, it is Workhouse Lane. Clearly, it took some time for the change of name to become established.

This narrow road leads to the playing field and is lined entirely by Feoffees owned houses. The current buildings are all fairly modern but the census of 1901 records eight residences. All of those cottages are now gone.

In 1907 the Parish Magazine reported the building of new Feoffees cottages:

In speaking of charity we hope everyone will take the opportunity of looking at our new Feoffees cottages. They are not expensive, look well, provided with every comfort for old people and built out of savings after fulfilling all the usual obligations to the parishioners. These three cottages will be occupied W Wilson and wife, R Cornwell and wife and Mrs Benton.

In 1915 the Feoffees considered that it was desirable to build a wash house to serve three cottages in School Lane.

Number 6 was designated as accommodation for the village nurse and Nurse Broadhead was a well-remembered resident.

School Lane in 1950 was reported to be in a bad state and Darby's of Sutton were asked to tender for the road to be tarred and gravelled or surfaced with tarmacadam. It was agreed to tar and gravel to a depth of one inch at a cost of five shillings per square yard. In the same year a letter was received asking for permission for it to be made a right of way for access to the proposed new recreation ground. Waiting for this decision was holding up the purchase of the land and the right of way was agreed to after a long discussion.

> *The Ives' garden was big, it was fairly wide and ran almost half way down School Lane, and then there were four (I think) elderly persons bungalows before the gate to the recreation field. Behind the school, opposite the elderly bungalows, there were two houses before the nurses house.*

In 1954 a tender of £2174 2s 7d was accepted from J. Acred to build a block of two almshouses and in the same year a suggestion was debated that a water supply and flush lavatories should be installed in School Lane.

The bungalows to the east of School Lane were recently built by the Feoffees.

Tower Road and Park Lane

Tower road is so named because it leads to Tower Farm, for discussion on a 'tower' see the Bishop's Palace. Park Lane borders the parkland attached to the Bishop's Palace. Early

> *Bert Gilbert – I always spoke to him when I walked past his tiny one storey dwelling in Tower Road.*

maps show no buildings in Tower Road and a row of agricultural labourers cottages in Park Lane and this was the situation right up to the 1911 census.

House building on Tower Road *Photo Courtesy David Bysouth*

John and Joyce lived at 10 Tower Road. John used to deal potatoes.

Development in Tower Road started with what are now numbers 3, 5, 7 and 9 in the 1920s. Subsequently,

Philip Bysouth built several houses here in 1945.

We originally lived at 10 Park Lane with the farm yard behind the entrance which came out adjacent to the Plough.

Townsend

Townsend is referred to in the court rolls of 1362 when Simon atte Townsend is named as a juror. However, the name Townsend seems to have fallen out of use and does not reappear again until the 1871 census. Prior to this various parts of Townsend are referred to as Hopkins Hill, near Hopkins Hill and Mill End. These areas are loosely defined as a family can be living at Mill End on one census and Hopkins Hill on the next without moving house. As the George and Dragon is sometimes at Mill End it would appear that the end of

Cannon Street was known as Hopkins Hill and the area facing Main Street was Mill End.

There are also more families listed as living at Hopkins Hill and Mill End than there appear to be houses for, so this area may have included parts of Main Street or Cannon Street.

There were two large ponds at the Cannon Street end of Townsend which would have been used for wetting cartwheels at the end of a day in the fields.

The following details can be gleaned from the 1939 register and other verifiable sources:

1 and 1A Townsend

Photo Courtesy Cambridgeshire Collection

These are a pair of new houses. Old Ordnance Survey maps show a square plot with a house in the north-east corner and outbuildings surrounding the plot. The 1939 register lists Herbert and Alice Crane as living here. Herbert describes himself as a smallholder and heavy worker and he was the son of William and Mary Crane who were the landlords of the Anchor pub.

2 and 3 Townsend

This pair of semi-detached houses appear on the 1900 Ordnance Survey map but the structures on the 1884 map have a different footprint so they were built between these two dates replacing older cottages.

Number 2 was the village police house and the best-remembered village policeman who lived here is Ginger Francis. In 1939 Robert Howard was the police constable who lived here with his wife Priscilla.

> Ginger Francis, I was terrified of going past his house with no lights on my bike.

> I am 60 years old and I can remember PC Freddie Page and I used to sit on his motorbike.

This became a private house when a new police house was built at 99 Main Street.

Arthur and Doris McAulliffe and family lived at number 3 in 1939 and Arthur was a permanent way labourer.

The first Police Constable recorded as living at Townsend is William Bennyworth in 1871. On all subsequent census returns up to and including 1911 there is only one house listed between the police house and the George and Dragon pub, which would suggest that one of these two properties has moved location.

4 Townsend

James and Gladys Spinks lived here in 1939. James was a smallholder. Arthur Spinks also lived here and he owned the windmill in Ely Road.

5 Townsend (Roseleigh)

In 1939 this was the home of the Terry family. Henrietta Terry, widow of Oliver Frank Terry, a carrier was living here with her daughter Rose Maud, and another relative Charles Terry.

6 Townsend (The Old George and Dragon)

It was built in the 19th century as a public house and the pub was up for sale in 1851 when it was occupied by Francis Cornwell. In 1904 the landlord of the George and Dragon was Abraham Hall when it was owned by A&B Hall of Ely, it had stabling for two horses and one vehicle. When it closed it was bought in 1936 by Emily Granfield from the then owner Cutlack and Harlock. A condition of the sale was that it would only be used as a private house. In 1939, Emily Granfield, listed as doing unpaid domestic duties, was living here with Owen Cole, a widowed farmer. Later on, Owen's son George Cole and his wife Joyce lived here. It is now the home of the Clarke family.

7 – 11 Townsend

These are all fairly new buildings built around the green that was once the pond. This area was previously a farmyard belonging to the Cole family, Owen Cole lived here after living at number 6. Alwyn Saberton also lived here as a farm labourer.

12 Townsend (The Old Bakery)

This house is remembered as Les Fryett's bakery.

In 1939 Elisha Saberton was living here and listed as incapacitated but his wife Emily was a confectioner and cake maker, Elisha had been a carpenter. There were also their two children, Cecil, who was a baker and poultry farmer and Brenda Eileen who, in 1946, married Les Fryett, who was already a confectioner, living at Lawn Lane. As well as a bakery Les ran a grocer's from here and Brenda ran the shop. Les would deliver bread and cakes around the village with big wicker baskets in the back of his van. It is currently owned by the Runciman family and let as a holiday cottage.

13 Townsend

In 1939 this was the home of Doris Baker, the widow of Ernest. Ernest was an engineer who was crushed to death by a traction engine in 1931. Doris was a Sunday school teacher at the Methodist chapel. It later became the home of the Lee family.

13A Townsend

Undeveloped in 1925, this plot is now the site of a modern house.

14 Townsend

This house is built on the site of outbuildings that were to the rear of number 15. They were demolished in 2005 to make way for development.

15 Townsend (Blacksmith's Cottage)

Here is a grade 2 listed building which is thought to date back to the early 1700s which gives it a claim, along with Bury House, to be the oldest house in the village. It is built on a long thin burgage plot which originally had a number of outbuildings to the rear. It is also thought to have been built on the footprint of an earlier building. The house has a medieval L-shaped town house layout originally with three sections, a parlour to the west, a secondary living area in the centre and a kitchen to the east. Subsequent additions have been made.

Early Ordnance Survey maps show a smithy at or near this house and the census returns list the Raynor family as blacksmiths living at Townsend. They owned the wheelwright business opposite, at what is now 102 Main Street, and may have had links with this cottage too.

My wife and I bought the cottage ten years ago as a dilapidated wreck and restored it. We sold it two years ago.

By 1939 Richard Gibson, former landlord of the Windmill pub was living here. Richard had also been a butcher and there are still signs of the butchers business in the house. Richard lived here with his wife, Kate, and six of their children. One son was Frederick 'Dobbie' Gibson who ran a shop in Main Street. The house was home to Richard's daughter Hilda for all except the last few months of her life. On her marriage to John Parrish, her parents passed the house to her. Originally thatched, the house was later roofed with corrugated iron, then finally with tiles.

Longmeadow

On the corner of Townsend and West Fen Drove this house is on land that in 1844 was owned by William Martin and then bought by William "Ginger" Moxon. The current house is the first on this site and was built in the mid-1950s. It was named Longmeadow after the field on which it stands and is currently owned by the Runciman family, descendants of William Moxon. The group of trees

152

immediately to the front of this house cover the site of the second, smaller pond at Townsend.

Whilst it is not possible to accurately assign people to properties from the old census returns it is worth looking at some of the families who lived at Townsend.

In 1939 Arthur, an ice cream salesman, and Clara Smith lived here.

There were several Hopkin/Hopkins (the names are interchangeable here) families that have lived here over the years. Philip Hopkins owned land to the East of West Fen Drove which probably gave rise to the name of Hopkins Hill. The first Hopkins recorded in the Little Downham parish registers is Richard Hopkins who married Alice Aspland in 1639, so Philip may have inherited the land from an earlier branch of the Hopkin family. Philip was born in Witchford and married Mary Hopkin in 1802 at Little Downham. Mary died in 1817 but Philip was living in Cannon Street in 1841 and died two years later.

By 1851 Joseph and Mary Hopkin were living at Hopkins Hill. Joseph was a farmer of 47 acres and the son of John and Elizabeth, there is no obvious relationship to Philip. In 1861 there three Hopkins families at Hopkins Hill and there remain Hopkins in this area through to the 1939 register.

In 1861 Rebecca Cole was running a grocer's shop at Townsend and by 1891 Ann Stevens was a grocer here. When Les Fryett was a baker at number 12 he also had a grocery although it is not clear whether these were all at the same premises.

Long term residents of Townsend were Gill and Lucy Cranfield who appear on all census returns between 1861 and 1901 and in that time they had thirteen children. Gill was a carpenter and died in 1916 aged 81. Lucy died in 1920 also aged 81.

Other names that have a long term association with this area are Cornwell, Waddelow, Moxon and Hancock.

White Horse Lane

Photo Courtesy Roy Crane

This is a small lane that runs off Cannon Street and is named after the pub that stood at the top of the lane. Old maps show a group of buildings at the bottom of the lane with a pump for water, so there may have been families living here but there are no houses listed in the census returns for White Horse Lane and the pub address is Cannon Street.

There are four landlords for The White Horse listed over time:
1851 Robert Webb
1861 to 1881 William Lofts
1891 Daniel Stevens
1904 John Frost. At this time it was owned by A & B Hall of Ely.
In 1957 number 3 White Horse Lane was sold for £1,350 along with outbuildings, orchard and arable land.

War Memorials

The war memorial is located in the churchyard at St Leonard's. The original inscription reads:

"To the glory of God and in grateful memory of those who went out from this parish and laid down their lives for us in the Great War, 1914-1918. Their name liveth for evermore."

It was dedicated in 1920 by the Bishop of Ely, Rt. Rev. F H Chase DD. The monument was presented to the parish by Mr George Darby of Pymoor and cost about £150. It was made by E. J. Case of King's Lynn.

The names recorded from the first war are: George Rumbelow, John Hill, Charles Fryett, Peter Cornwell, Harry Missin, Edward L J Stockdale, Walter James Pearson, Solomon Thorpe, Jacob Arthur Peacock, Albert Edward Barrett, John Jordan, George Garner, Alfred William Carter, Horace William Green, John William Goudge, John William Rudderham, Percy W J Cornwell, Archer Saberton, Thomas William Swain, Frederick Harrison, Abraham Martin, Herbert Martin, Horace L Wright, Alfred Taylor, Henry Culpin, Arthur H Smith, Albert Harrison, Alexander Cornwell, Charles B Fincham, Alexander Tingey, Albert Martin, Joseph V Saberton.

The names of those who died in the second war were later added as follows: Eddie Bailey, Arthur Arnold Bidwell, Bernard Crane, Frank Frost, Archie Jefferson, Ronald George Missin, Stanley Nicholas, Ernest Victor Yardy.

A second gate was made into the churchyard so that non-conformists could attend the war memorial without using the main entrance to the church.

There was also a men's club built as a memorial (see Main Street).

A plaque has been erected in front of the village hall to commemorate a first war landing ground situated in the area of Tower Farm.

Recreation Ground

The original recreation ground was on the field next to the current one, now Edward Runciman's grass field. It had football pitches and crude facilities for the players. The land was owned by F. G. W. Darby and in 1942 he put it up for sale. It was sold as part of a parcel of land described as 21acres 3 roods and 37 poles of rich old pasture land about eight acres of which formed the recreation ground and was bought by the Manchester Unity of Oddfellows, Little Downham, for £1,200.

> *Was it Frank or Henry that donated the old wooden cricket pavilion? I was told that it was originally a chicken shed. I remember having a few teas in there when dad used to play cricket. It burnt down and I remember watching the fire engine driving down the field and putting the fire out.*

The current site was originally called Cook's Field and had a pond just inside the gate which stretched up to the allotments. In summer it was a dipping pond for newts and in the winter a skating rink. In 1948 it was reported that Little Downham Parish Council approved a £1400 scheme for the provision of a recreation ground to include football and cricket pitches, tennis courts, bowling green, children's corner and a pavilion. Half of the cost was met by the Ministry of Education with the rest raised through public subscription.

Libraries

Little Downham was served for many years by a mobile library but in 1967 a shop previously occupied by the Co-op was leased for use as a library. It contained over 1,000 books and was considered to be a trial for branch libraries in small communities. This library was later replaced by a prefabricated building in the village hall car park which closed in the 1990s and the County Library Service reverted to a mobile library. Following an offer from the proprietor of the Convenience Store/Post Office at 59 Main Street, a smaller facility enabled a basic exchange service to be reopened in 1996 as the 'Bookcase'; this was a few shelves of books in the Store that were regularly exchanged on a monthly basis with new stock from Cambridgeshire Libraries. The facility worked well for a couple of years until there was a change of proprietor. Sadly, the books were then not regularly changed on the shelves with the new monthly issues and Cambridgeshire Libraries frequently complained that statistics were not being properly maintained.

Following negotiations by Little Downham Parish Council in 1999 the Little Downham Book Café idea was developed and formally opened in October 2000 under the leadership of Derek and Helen Last. Derek and other volunteers made the shelving and other required fittings and displays. After much negotiation, the County Library Service agreed to provide books and allow it to access the County Library facilities. As the venture proved a success the Library Service used it as a model to encourage other communities to establish and manage their own local facilities.

Little Downham Book Café was the first of its kind in the country and was mentioned as this by Members of Parliament in Westminster. It is hailed as a flagship for what is now known as Local Access Point and during its first five years was visited by a Member of Parliament, County, District and Parish Councillors to see how it was set up for other communities to follow.

OXLODE

Oxlode is a small hamlet lying at the end of Adventurers Drove. The Adventurers were the engineers and wealthy sponsors who paid towards the project of fen drainage in the seventeenth century and who then claimed large tracts of the reclaimed land. Their enterprise is remembered in the Adventurers droves and fens that bear their name around the fens. Oxlode has dwindled to a small group of houses at the end of the drove as Pymoor has increased in size.

Adventurers drove would once have been the route of the main road between Manea and Little Downham and onwards to Ely, passing through Oxlode and Purles Bridge. Thomas Yeakell's map of 1810 shows the course of the road between the Hundred Foot River and the River Delph and this would doubtless have been used as a highway after these rivers were dug for drainage, with ferries across the rivers only gradually falling out of use. The diaries of Richard Taylor, Curate of Coveney, recalls his journey across the washes to Manea in 1833. This shows that Oxlode was still an important waypoint when travelling to Manea and it demonstrates that he used ferries or rode his horse across the river and how difficult the wash crossing could be:

I took a funeral at Manea and found the fen very wet, the water being level with the land and the roads very bad. The water was in the wash more than three feet deep in the shallowest place and the wind rendered the passage very stormy…

My ferryman of Parl's Bridge sent me a present of a heron-shaw…

I did the duty at Manea in the morning riding my mare through the river at Oxlode and taking her on to Manea and thence rode on by Mepal and Witcham where I preached for the first time……

Once on returning to Coveney from Manea with Mr Fisk, it was a little late and the ferryman had gone to bed. The two of them spent almost an hour shouting at the tops of their voices from the far bank in order to rouse him!

Another extract from Richard Taylor's diary describes his encounter with a will-o-the-wisp that he had on the fen:

I got benighted being a very cloudy night and no moon. I never remembered seeing it so dark and it was with the greatest difficulty I managed to find my way as I could neither distinguish the road or the ditches. When I got to Oxlode, old Forman lent me a large black oak stick which I found of the greatest service as it enabled me to feel my way. When I got to Wayhead I saw what I fancied was a lanthorn a little way off, so I walked through thick and thin (for the mud was nearly ancle deep all the way) to get up to it but without appearing to gain upon it. I then stopped and listened whether I could hear the footsteps of the person who carried the light and was then surprised to see it dance first to one side of the road to the other and back again in a moment. I was much pleased as I got so near as distinctly to see its shape. It kept appearing and disappearing every moment, and I observed it several times divide itself into two parts leaving a streak of light between and then come together again. I stood still and it appeared to move towards me. In fact it seemed to come quite close and so rapidly as to rather startle me. It was then a round light as large as the full moon. I afterwards saw another. This light does not appear to me to be inflammable gas as is generally supposed arising from the oily particles of decomposed aquatic plants, but simply luminous air or phosphoric light arising from the drains, the same as I have seen rotten wood emit a very strong light in the night. The ignus fatuus (will-o-the-wisp) is only seen on the darkest nights. I believe the one I saw came so near as actually to touch my face.

Within living memory, cattle have been swum across the river at Oxlode to summer pasture on the Washes.

As the use of this route to Manea has fallen out of use the community of Oxlode has dwindled and Pymoor has increased in size to become the larger of the two hamlets. Oxlode was a stopping place for barges on the Hundred Foot river and early Ordnance Survey maps show towpaths along each bank of the river. The rise in the railways caused a decline in barge traffic, again leading to the decline of the hamlet.

This route was considered important enough to warrant second world war defences to be built guarding Adventurers Drove. They were part of a defence line that ran from Ramsey Forty Foot, around the north of Littleport and followed the River Lark to Bury St. Edmunds. There are two type 28 and one type 28a anti-tank gun emplacements. There is another anti-tank gun emplacement by the bank to the west of Straight Drove.

The name of Oxlode is thought to be a contraction of Ox-willow Lode and I have seen one suggestion that it was once called Foxlode.

Like most of the parish outside the main village of Little Downham Oxlode is an agricultural community and the residents have been almost entirely farmers and agricultural workers. There are a few exceptions in 1841: William Meadows, a confectioner; James Mason, a blacksmith and John Harvard, a glazier.

In August 1804 Thomas Nicholas, a shopkeeper of Oxlode, was fined by the Inspector of Weights and Measures for having weights deficient at one stone, one pound and half a pound.

William and Mary Harrison are listed as shopkeepers living here in 1871 and twenty years later James Harrison was a grocer. Presumably, they ran their business in Oxlode.

In 1869 the farm where Bays Farm now stands at the end of Adventurers Drove was up for sale and described as follows:

All that freehold farmhouse, with a barn, cart horse stable, granary, cow lodge, calves' place, hen house and hay lodge and a newly erected timber and tiled nag stable, with two loose boxes, drill house, piggery, firing lodge and waggon lodge, together with 13a 0r 20p of freehold pasture and arable land adjoining.

Byall Fen Farm was up for sale in 1949, including the farmhouse. It was a substantial building with a similar list of outbuildings as other farm sales. There is an interesting list of items that the tenant claimed as theirs: the bath, flush pedestal lavatory, hot water cistern, cold water supply tank, airing cupboard, water supply pipes in bath room, the Ideal Domestic Boiler in the scullery and the electrical fittings. As it was advertised with imminent vacant possession presumably the tenant intended to take all the plumbing and electrical fittings with them. Today the farmhouse is derelict.

The Feoffees minutes for May 1954 include a proposal to build a bridge across the washes at Oxlode. Owners of about half the land affected agreed to support the scheme and contribute about 60% of the capital required. However, these plans came to nothing.

Water Mill

In 1790 a water mill was advertised for sale by auction at the Club Inn, Ely. It was called Oxlode Mill, standing on the Hundred Foot Bank.

Another advert was placed in the newspapers in April 1840 stating that it was of interest to millwrights and others:

```
To be sold by private contract, a good timbered
water mill, carrying a 22 feet sail, now standing
on the 17th Interior District in Downham Fen, near
Oxlode.

Inquire of John Upsher, jun, at Oxlode, in
Downham, In the Isle of Ely.
```

William Farrow was a miller living at Oxlode in 1871 and William's wife Mary Keech Farrow was a schoolmistress.

Methodist Chapel

The Methodist Weslyan Chapel was established in 1836 and rebuilt in 1878. It stood on the bank at the end of the footpath from School Lane in Pymoor. In the 1881 census, Thomas Golding was a cordwainer and Methodist lay preacher.

Cyril Heaps remembers the chapel: As you entered into this lovely old building the aisle went round each side of the chapel, the oak stained boards about four feet high were fixed to the walls and a tortoise stove stood halfway down the left side of the building. The organ was an old harmonium (now in the vestry of Pymoor chapel) on the left side of the chapel with choir pews between the organ and the pulpit with more pews the other side of the pulpit. The communion rail was of wood fixed to curved iron stays and a communion table in the centre.

Cyril also mentions that the chapel was built in 1845 which contradicts the earlier date that has been sourced.

The chapel fell out of use when a new chapel was built in Pymoor and its remains are in the garden of Wakes Cottage.

Pubs

There were two pubs in Oxlode, the Crown and the Three Horseshoes. On early census returns the publicans are listed but it does not say which landlord served at which pub. In 1841 John Foreman was a publican at the age of 80 and may well be the gentleman that lent Richard Taylor a large, black, oak stick. John Foreman was succeeded by John Canham who remained a publican and farmer at the 1871 census. Mendham and Mary Martin were at the other pub and were succeeded by James Butcher.

In 1835 Mr Chapman wrote to the Bedford Level Corporation as follows:

```
I will engage to build a new house at Oxlode at
the sign of the Three Horse Shoes and repair the
two old tenements to join with the new one, to be
slated and to be done in workmanship in a manner
according to Mr Joseph Little's orders for the sum
of 150 pounds.
```

Joseph Little was a surveyor for the Bedford Level Corporation and reported on the state of the public houses owned by the corporation around this time. The Crown was in good order but the Three Horseshoes was in a bad state, the house falling down, stables very bad and thatch of part of the house bad. Unless something is done part of the house must soon be down.

In 1854 the Bedford Level corporation leased the Crown to brewers John and Henry Hall for four years at a rent of £50 a year. In 1881 Russel Pate was the landlord and then Albert Dewsberry took over. By 1904 the Crown was owned by A & B Hall of Ely, the landlord was Frederick Taylor and it had stabling for eight horses.

In 1881 William Taylor was landlord of the Three Horseshoes followed by William Young. Moses Heaps had been a stationary engine driver and then became landlord of the Three Horseshoes and the pub was owned by the Bedford Level Corporation who leased it to Morgans Brewery of Norwich.

The Heaps family later became landlords of the Crown (now a private house named Mandalay). There is a story that Reuben Bailey moved in with the Heaps by coming home from school with one of the children and then just stayed. Reuben was born 22 December 1916 and had a brother, Walter, who in 1939 was a land worker living with the Powers family on the 100ft bank, probably working at Phoenix Farm. Their parents were Walter and Mabel Bailey who lived at Straight Furlong. Reuben died in 1997.

Eva Heaps bought the building in 1940 with a commitment to cease running it as a pub.

Oxlode Manor

Oxlode Manor was a large house by the bank and Cyril Heaps reports that it was first recorded in 1732 as home to the Leaford family. The remains of the servants quarters now stand in the grounds of Oxlode Fishing Lakes.

in the late 1800s, the Manor was home to the Norman family but it has not featured sufficiently in the written records to determine other residents.

Harry Cross, a farm labourer and his wife Mary lived in quarters attached to the Manor House followed by the Hannahs, who were the last family to live there.

FEBRUARY 2nd. 1951.

OXLODE PATH REPAIRS

"SERIOUS STATE"

County Council Approached

THE BAD STATE OF THE OXLODE PATH — the only road which children in the area can use on their way to and from Pymoor school—came in for discussion at a meeting of Downham Parish Council on Monday, when it was agreed that the Isle County Council be asked to effect repairs.

Held in the School, the meeting was presided over by Coun. A. W. Chambers.

Coun. A. E. Bidwell reported that the path was in such a serious state of disrepair that during the recent bad weather it had been almost impossible for children, who were the principal users, to get to school.

Other members complained of the disgraceful state of the path and expressed surprise that the children had, in fact, attended school.

Indignation was expressed that the adequate repair of the path, which was beyond the power of the Council, had been neglected so long, in view of its importance to the inhabitants of Oxlode.

JUNE 15, 1951

OXLODE PATH

Presenting the report of the Oxlode Path Committee, Coun. Chambers said that he, with Couns. Darby and Harrison, had met the County Surveyor and that agreement had been reached concerning the resurfacing of the path. The County Surveyor said that the path would be surfaced from the Church to Oxlode. Tarmac would be used for the surfacing and the width of the path would be three feet. It was also agreed to apply a permanent dressing to the road from Pymoor to the Church.

164

John Heaps remembers Oxlode: In the sixties the Oxlode Methodist Chapel was gone and the manor was a ruin. The house going towards the Crown was where Charlie Norman lived and I think is still there. The next house was where Nellie Cross lived, she moved into Pymoor to become housekeeper for Bertie Pearson, then Reg Wake's house, hence it is called Wakes Cottage. I think that these houses were bought by birdwatchers for holiday homes. The bungalow at Bay's Farm was built for Jack Heaps, then there was the former Crown Pub.

Oxlode Pumping Station

In 1962 Lord de Ramsey, President of the Association of Drainage Authorities, formally opened their new pumping station at Oxlode, which uses electric motors.

The ceremony was preceded by a luncheon held, appropriately, in the Club Hotel, Ely where, in 1756, the Littleport and Downham Drainage Commissioners held their first meeting. There the toast to the Littleport and Downham District was proposed by the Chairman of the Great Ouse River Board, who recalled something of the Board's progressive history. After operating for about 30 years they had erected a steam engine with a scoop wheel, something very modern in those days. After 60 years they came to diesel and centrifugal pumps and now, some 40 years later, he congratulated them on putting in the very modern pump at Oxlode.

The River Board had been the Commissioners' consultants for the erection of the new pumping station, and he sincerely hoped the advice they had given had been satisfactory and that their work would be of great benefit to the farmers of the area for many years to come.

The Chairman turned to the River Board's Flood Protection Scheme which, it was hoped, would be completed in time for any winter flood in 1963. He was very pleased with it but said it was too early for them to be too cocksure as to what would be its result.

They had, however, been delighted with the ways they had been able to control water in the Ten Mile during the last winter when water did not get more than six inches above summer level. Had the same amount of water been coming down without the help of the relief channel it would have been between 109 and 110 inches. That would have meant seepage through the banks and pumping water over and over again.

The speaker realised the cost of the scheme would be a burden on the Littleport and Downham Board for possibly the next 40 or 50 years, but they had been unfortunate with regard to the rate of interest on money they had had to borrow. It had risen from 3 percent in 1954 to 6¾ percent. Nevertheless, he was quite sure anything they paid for the cost of the scheme they would save in the reduced pumping they would have to do.

Replying, the Chairman of the commissioners told the gathering that the idea for the Oxlode Pump was first discussed by the Committee of the authority in 1940, when there was a tremendous drive for increased agricultural production, and the River Board lowered the channel bringing water from Grunty Fen into the district between

166

2000 and 3000 acres. Permission for the new pump was not given and the 100 foot pump was altered to take the water.

Total cost of the new pumping station would be £65,000 and the Commissioners appreciated the help of the Ministry of Agriculture towards the outlay. The chairman also informed his listeners that the Commissioners were asking the River Board to build two more pumping stations, one at Denver Sluice and the other between Littleport and Ely.

The lunch over, the gathering adjourned to the site of the new pumping station at Oxlode, where Lord de Ramsey was introduced by the chairman who gave Lord de Ramsey the key to the building and the visitor entered and pressed the switch which set the pumps working, and water from the drain pouring into the outfall so swiftly that onlookers could see the water level fall.

Hitherto the district had had only two pumping stations. Now they had a third and two more were contemplated in the future. The addition of the new Oxlode station meant it would be possible to divide the area nearly equally into three parts of 10,000 acres each. That would be a big improvement to the low-lying area in the south-east which was beginning to suffer from poor drainage, due to the gradual wastage of the peat. Some of the water from the Byall and West Fen had to travel seven miles to reach the 100 foot.

Turning to engineering Lord de Ramsey pointed out that the district was already three to four feet below sea level and could shrink up to a further four feet. In addition there had been two physical constructions or obstructions, the Skew Bridge under the March/Ely railway line, and the ridge of highland which necessitated a deep cut, known as the Dunkirk cut, which it was impossible to deepen further. Oxlode provided the shortest possible route for water from those Fens to the 100 foot. The reduced area served by the 100 foot would, he said, continue to link with Oxlode so the new station would be able to help out under flood conditions.

The station had been designed and constructed by the River Board at a cost of £48,000, and the drain works were carried out by the Board's own labour and plant at a cost of £17,000. Lord de Ramsey went on to say that two mixed flow 36/39 inch diameter pumps were driven by 320 b.h.p. motors, delivering 270 tons of water a minute against a static head of 20ft. The pumps had been made by Messrs Hathorn Davey and Co. Ltd.

In 1963 the ice was so thick that dynamite had to be used to clear the valves on the river.

08 January 2013

Broken drainage pumps led to dramatically high levels of water in Pymoor drain

Staff worked round the clock to monitor the situation and rake out weed, while local farmers helped set up temporary pumps and were the "eyes and ears" of the Littleport and Downham Drainage Board. Board engineer Andrew Newton said: "Between December 19 and the new year we had two-and-a-half inches of rain, and unfortunately we were down on capacity, so it was very dramatic. People are saying it was the highest water level they had ever known. We pump the water into the Hundred Foot Drain, some nearby fields were waterlogged, but no properties were flooded."

PYMOOR

The spelling of the name of this hamlet has been a matter of dispute over the years but I will default to Pymoor. On Thomas Yeakell's map of 1810 it is spelt Pyemoor and on the 1900 Ordnance Survey map as Pymore.

In 1974 the Post Office made a decision: Little Downham Parish Council complained that someone somewhere had put an extra "O" in the spelling of the village name; now that "O" has been knocked out. So now Pymoor will be known as Pymore, officially at least.

The GPO have reverted to the "'ore" spelling on their franking machine and the change of spelling has been cleared by the County Council. Mrs Florence Brown, postmistress at Pymoor for 18 years, says that the majority of people of the village spell the name with two O's. " I have lived in the village all my life and Pymore has always been known as Pymoor," explained 68-year-old Mrs Brown.

"Double "O" is certainly the most popular, but I suppose people will still spell it the same as they always did and I'm sure they will not take any notice of what the officials say."

Mrs Claude Golding, President of the village Women's Institute, has warned all her members of the change." I have tried to find out the history of the name and the correct spelling but have been unable to," she explained. "It is all very confusing."

In 1980 the spelling came up for discussion again: The unveiling of a village sign will clear up an argument which has raged for years. Ancient records show that the hamlet was named Pimore but over the years it had become either Pymore or Pymoor, according to fancy. Most local people spell it "OOR" but the clerk of Little Downham Parish Council says he used "ORE" and always will do. Two signs in the village spell it differently.

But now a new wooden sign has been carved, reading Pymoor. It will be unveiled at Pymoor Hill. The name means 'flies over a bog'.

The question was put to the vote in January 1997 when the Parish Council declared that the name on the sign was indeed the correct one.

As the locals pronounce it Pymah, the spelling is perhaps academic.

The centre of Pymoor is the crossroads where all the roads meet. Coming in from the south is Main Street, heading east is Pymoor Lane, north-east is Straight Furlong and south-west is School Lane leading to Pygore. The area around this crossroads is known as Pymoor Hill.

The Feoffees own two cottages in Pymoor and have always historically had properties in the hamlet. In 1872 they put houses up for sale described as a pair of modern brick-built and tiled cottages in the occupation of William Bell and Richard Biggs, reserve price £230. These were on Main Street near the corner with Pymoor Lane. The Feoffees currently own 7 and 9 Main Street. In 1944 it was agreed to build brick lavatories for the cottages but this decision was rescinded as too expensive in favour of portable wooden lavatories but in 1946 it was reported that the requirement for two wash houses and two lavatories was most necessary.

Frith Head Drove is now a byway with Dunkirk Farm the only house there, however, the 1861 census has six entries for Frith Head Drove, all agricultural workers. The Feoffees owned a farm here and in 1867 it was recorded in the minutes that Spooner's House at Frith Head needed to be rebuilt. The house in Frith Head Drove continually appeared in the minute books as requiring repair until 1967 when it was decided to sell the property along with six acres of land.

Again the census returns show that Pymoor was the home mainly to agricultural workers with the population increasing and occupations becoming more varied with time.

It was reported in the local newspaper that electricity came to Pymoor in 1954 and was switched on by P. H. Stevens, J. P. at a ceremony held at the Methodist church schoolroom. Street lights followed in 1960.

Pubs

Between 1841 and 1861 John Stevens was a publican in Pymoor succeeded in the 1871 census by William Seekins.

In 1881 there were two publicans: William Seekins at the Wheatsheaf and George Shaw at the Knife and Steel. Ten years later William Seekins was a farmer and John Moxon was the only publican at the Knife and Steel. This indicates that the original pub in Pymoor was the Wheatsheaf which fell out of use and the Knife Steel became the only pub. In 1904 Charles Wiseman was the landlord and it was owned by Abraham Stevens of Upwell. Later on, William Jordan was the landlord.

The Knife and Steel is now a private house, number 4 Main Street. After it closed as a pub it was bought by Graham and Kath Lark who sold it to the Barker family who are the current owners. The Wheatsheaf was close by on the opposite side of the street.

Shops and Businesses

The first record of a shop in Pymoor is Philip Nicholas who was a grocer in 1871 and thirty years later Emily Fretwell was a shopkeeper.

Charlie Brown in front of Pymoor Post office
Photo Courtesy Cyril Heaps

The post office has been in several locations over the years. The picture above was number one Main Street, on the corner with Pymoor Lane. Some of the later locations were on

Barkers on the corner of Main Street and School Lane, where you could get everything you needed.

Mr Barker had a garage that sold fuel and did bike repairs – you said in money how much fuel you wanted and Mr Barker rang the guage round to that amount and the fuel was pumped out and the guage ran backwards.

the opposite side of the road at Barker's Store, at number six Pymoor Lane and the old windmill in Pymoor Lane.

In 1953 a house called Crossways, on the corner of Pymoor Lane and Straight Furlong was put up for sale by Mr F. G. W. Darby. There was a house, garden, farm buildings and a lot of poultry sheds. It was inhabited by Mr E. D. Barker who had given an undertaking to move out.

Just around the corner, on the north side of Pymoor Lane, was a Smithy with William Stevens and later Simon Ashman being recorded as blacksmiths in Pymoor.

There have been two shops in Pymoor within living memory, Barker's and Saberton's.

Barker's (A. S. Barker and Son) was a petrol station and a shop on the corner of Main Street and School Lane. It opened in 1913 and is now replaced by a private house. Ted Barker, who owned the shop was an A.R.P. warden during the war.

The other shop was Saberton's which was started by Hugh Saberton. Hugh was a blacksmith who lived next to the shop at number 11 Main Street, now called the Old Blacksmiths House, and started with a blacksmith business at the rear of the old shop building. The shop opened in 1921 and concentrated on selling bicycles but soon expanded to groceries too. Hugh married and moved to Cottenham to start another shop and Hugh's brother, Horace (Horry), took on the business in 1937. Their sister Vera helped out behind the counter while Horry was away in the war. Vera

Coronation Medal for Pymoor Man

SUB-POSTMASTER FOR 50 YEARS

AMONG those of the district's personalities awarded the Queen's Coronation Medal is Mr. Frederick C. Brown, Sub-postmaster at Pymoor, who received the medal on Coronation morning.

Now in his fiftieth year as Sub-postmaster at Pymoor, Mr. Brown has seen many changes. Among them was the metalling of soft droves, along which he once had to make a ten-mile walk in his daily mail deliveries.

Mr. Brown served in Queen Victoria's forces, seeing action in the Boer War under the late Lord Methuen. His brother, Mr. J. Brown, another soldier of that war, also lives in Pymoor-lane, and still enjoys fairly good health.

remained in the shop until it closed in 1986 when the rise in supermarkets made the business unviable.

A sales poster from 1887 advertises a blacksmith's and wheelwright's shop for sale situated in Main Street. Another sales poster from 1894 advertises two cottages, blacksmith's and carpenter's shops and buildings occupied by L. D. Seekings and J. Stevens.

Saberton's Store, Main Street in 2020

Pymoor Lane

In 1909 a test case was brought to court to determine whether or not Pymoor Lane was a public highway. George Martin, Thomas Gillett and Jacob Peacock appeared before Ely magistrates for allowing cattle to stray in Pymoor Lane. Following P. C. Challis's testimony the magistrate asked "Is Pymoor Lane a highway?" to which the policeman replied "Yes; with a metalled road extending for a mile … although he didn't know the state of the road 40 or 50 years ago". He went on to say that he didn't know who made the road or who metalled it. He considered that it was a highway because he had seen the public walk and drive over it. The Lane was a link between Westmoor Common and Fodder Fen Common. Both commons and Pymoor Lane were all open unenclosed land, private property abutted on each side of Pymoor Lane. There was a hedge in some places and a dyke in others. Mr Bendall for the defence said that he could prove for a great number of years back the two commons had been used by the people of Little Downham for the purpose of their horses and cattle being turned out there.

In Little Downham, under the enclosure award, there was a person called a pinder, whose duty it was to see that stock did not travel on to the highway. The pinder has been superseded and the police now exercised this duty.

The case for the defence was that the lane had originally been a green drove that was used for driving cattle and metalling the road did not change the status of the Lane in law. However, the magistrate declared that Pymoor Lane was a highway and the defendants were each fined one shilling and seven shillings costs.

Windmills and bakers

There were two corn mills in Pymoor a hundred years ago and several bakers and millers listed in the census. One windmill was located to the west of Main Street on the corner of the CN Seeds site. The other still stands in Pymoor Lane and is now a private residence.

The first recorded miller is William Fretwell from Wereham, Norfolk (he married a local girl) listed as a master baker and grocer, which suggests that he had a shop, but by 1871 he was listed as

Possibly Pymoor Main Street Windmill.
Photo Courtesy Cambridgeshire Collection

a miller. In 1891 his son Henry had taken on the business as baker and miller, with an assistant Henry Eno from Lincolnshire.

ALL THAT WAS LEFT AFTER £700 PYMOOR FIRE.

The old windmill at Pymoor Lane was the home of Darby's miller and baker. The Darby family were primarily millers and farmers who employed bakers which may account for the many bakers recorded in the census as living in Pymoor. The Darbys started baking in the 1890s and they first appear in the Little Downham census records as millers in 1891 and in the 1896 street directory for Pymoor, George Darby is listed as a miller (steam and wind). George was succeeded by his son Francis George, the first Darby baptised in the parish. In 1932 they opened a shop in Ely which sported the only electric sign in the city when it opened. In 1936 the bakery had a fire, reported in the newspaper of the time:

"A fire, which caused damage amounting to £700, lasted about two and a half hours on Saturday morning at a Pymoor bakery owned by Mr F. G. W.

Darby, who trades as Messrs G. Darby and Son. The fire was discovered just before six o'clock when a confectioner in the bakehouse noticed smoke coming from a hole in the wall from the confectionery department. When he opened the door, he saw that the department was on fire and thick clouds of smoke made it impossible for him to go into the building. An attempt was made to put the fire out with an extinguisher, but it was found that the outbreak was rapidly getting out of control, and the confectioner went for Mr Darby, who sent for help from the village and telephoned for Ely fire Brigade, who arrived within 20 minutes of receiving the call. The cause of the outbreak is thought to have been that the fat which was to have been used to fry doughnuts caught on fire. The confectionery department was soon gutted, only the cake mixing

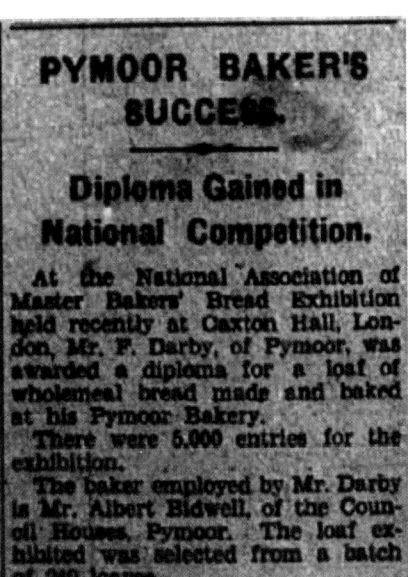

PYMOOR BAKER'S SUCCESS.

Diploma Gained in National Competition.

At the National Association of Master Bakers' Bread Exhibition held recently at Caxton Hall, London, Mr. F. Darby, of Pymoor, was awarded a diploma for a loaf of wholemeal bread made and baked at his Pymoor Bakery.

There were 5,000 entries for the exhibition.

The baker employed by Mr. Darby is Mr. Albert Bidwell, of the Council Houses, Pymoor. The loaf exhibited was selected from a batch of 240 loaves.

machine being saved, and even this will have to be reconditioned before it can be used. The fire then spread to the room where two grist milling machines were placed. The heat was so terrific that the four stones, two weighing one ton each and the other two half a ton each, were cracked and broken in several pieces. The wooden stairs were soon in flames, and a few minutes later the wooden floor collapsed, and with it came several tons of provisions. As far as is known, there were about 55 coombes of maize, 40 cwts of meal mash and 30 cwts of meal. The roof of the stores caved in 10 minutes after the fire was discovered, which gives some idea of the way the flames spread. Meanwhile, the rafters of the bakehouse had caught alight, and slates were torn off the roof so that water could be poured onto them. It was only by a superhuman effort on the part of the employees and villagers that the flames were overcome and the bakehouse was saved. Hardly had this part of the outbreak been brought under control than it was seen that the door of the engine room was alight, and flames were licking the walls and rafters. Machinery worth several hundred pounds, as well as about 1000 gallons of fuel oil were in danger, but fortunately the flames were overcome, though not until it was only a few feet from the machinery. The electrical switchboard in an adjoining room was absolutely ruined, but the accumulators were saved. The brigade had the fire under control about 7 o'clock, but it was not until 8:30 that all danger was passed. In the confectionery department, all the utensils were destroyed, and 500 loaves of bread were spoilt. The fire did not spread to the mill, which was only a few feet away from the engine room, but the heat was so intense that the tar on the mill walls was melted. Mr Darby said that at one time he had given up hope of any of the buildings being saved, and but for the work of the brigade, and the villagers, particularly the lady helpers, the damage must have been considerably greater. The firm have been carrying on a bakery business for the past 40 years, but it was not until 15 months ago that it was decided to venture into the confectionery side. They now deliver all over Ely district and employ 10 men, who are working night and day to cope with orders."

As can be seen from Albert Bidwell's success the business recovered but closed in Pymoor in the 1950s.

The windmill was increased in height in 1898 and worked into the 1930s. By 1995 the sails and cap had been removed and it was being used as the Post Office. It is now a private house.

Carnival and sports day

Pymoor Carnival was a long-standing tradition which seems to have started as a sports day and became something bigger. It was being reported as a carnival in the local paper in 1933 and still going in the 1970s. In 1999 Pymoor held an agricultural show, which became a major event attracting businesses from around the country and large crowds. The pressure of organising the event led to its demise when the 2012 show had to be cancelled because of torrential rain.

MAY 14, 1920.

PYMOOR AND OXLODE SPORTS.

The above Sports will be held on **TUESDAY, JUNE 8th,** IN A FIELD (Kindly lent by Mr. G. Darby).

Upwards of **£80** will be spent in Prizes, &c.

THE **MAHEA SILVER PRIZE BAND** WILL BE IN ATTENDANCE.

Several Open Cycle and Flat Racing Events.

Application for Entrance Forms to be made to E. W. Smith, Pymoor.

School and Church

Holy Trinity Church and school were built under the auspices of the Reverend Frederick Fisher in 1865 on land provided by Clare College, Cambridge. It stands on a footpath running from School Lane to Oxlode Lakes and was intended to be convenient for both Pymoor and Oxlode. The building was designed by Lewis Thompson of Wisbech and Edward Browne, Bishop of Ely, presided at the opening ceremony on 21st July 1865. As the school increased in numbers the building was extended in 1913. The school closed In July 1981 and the last service was held in the church on Christmas day 1981. The font and bell were given to Pymoor

Methodist Chapel and the bell stands in a brick cradle in front of the Chapel. Holy Trinity is now a private house.

The school was inspected in 1881:

This little fen school is difficult to work on account of the scattered character of the population. The present mistress works energetically and has achieved very fair success. The reading is fluent but without intonation. The writing and spelling are fair and the arithmetic weak.

In 1885 there was a proposal that two Feoffees cottages in Pymoor be appropriated for use as a school. However, this was rejected because it would reduce the value of the buildings.

Pymoor Methodist Chapel

Pymoor Methodist Chapel was the vision of Harold Fletcher, the village postman. The original chapel was by the river bank, part of Oxlode. Harold thought that more people would attend chapel if it was more conveniently sited. Money raising commenced in 1947 with doorstep collections across the fens and garden fetes. The foundation stone was laid in 1953 (it rained all day) and the Chapel opened on 29th June 1954.

NEW METHODIST CHURCH AT PYMOOR

ON THE FEN

Downham Hythe

A hythe is a landing place or small port for ships or boats and there was a lode here between Little Downham and Wayhead. The origin of this waterway is not specifically recorded but it is first mentioned in records in the first half of the 13th century and was probably instigated by the Bishop of Ely. Records of goods transported on the waterway show that it travelled northwards from the Hythe towards Manea and onwards to Chatteris. The drainage of the fens was a major change of the landscape and waterways were created whilst others disappeared. Therefore it is no longer possible to determine the exact route of this lode. Downham Hythe now refers to an area of the parish with some interesting place names: Otterbush, Redcaps and Landfloods.

Otterbush Farm is in Redcaps Lane. Redcap is an alternative name for a goldfinch which may explain the name. Otterbush has been recorded with several spellings including Otrebush and Attarbush but the origin of the name is unknown.

Landfloods Drove runs from Guildacre to the Hythe and is marked on old maps as a major road but is now a grass drove. The name would seem to be self-explanatory. It does not appear as a location on the census returns.

The 1851 census lists nine houses at the Hythe with one uninhabited. Over the years the residents have all been farmers and farm labourers with the exception of Thomas Jefferson who, in 1851, was a retailer of beer although no pubs are recorded here.

Also in 1851, Otterbush Farm was the home of Jeremiah Sandford a farmer of 230 acres employing 6 labourers. Subsequent census returns show a different resident each time sometimes farmers and sometimes agricultural labourers and farm bailiffs.

The Droves

This covers a large part of the north-east of the parish which includes Fodder Fen, Downham Common and Head Fen. It is an agricultural landscape with the occasional small business operating from a farmyard or house. A cursory glance at any early map shows a large number of small fields bounded by drainage ditches, a legacy of the drainage of the Fens which began in the 1630s.

Third Drove was surfaced for 33 chains in 1905 and fourth Drove was surfaced in the same year.

Census returns list almost entirely farmers, agricultural labourers, mole catchers and railway workers. There were always turfmen in the Droves and turf is still grown here today.

In 1871 George Cheesewright is a general shopkeeper living in Second Drove although it not clear whether his shop was here or elsewhere. It is the only reference to any shop in the Droves.

FRIDAY, MAY 3rd, 1963

OLD 'DOG & GUN' SOLD

THE FORMER "Dog and Gun" public house in Second-drove, Little Downham, together with five acres of fen land, was sold for £1,700 on Thursday week.

In 1851 Henry Casbourn was a beerhouse keeper in Fourth Drove although the name of the pub is not recorded and he was succeeded ten years later by Edward Smith. This is the last reference to a pub in Fourth Drove.

The Dog and Gun was a pub on Second drove and the first recorded landlord was George Smith. George was succeeded by William Hobbs of Soham and then Robert Jordan who was a publican and farmer. It was owned by William Cutlack, brewers of

Littleport. Robert died in 1914 age 82 and his son George took on the pub. In 1939 George's widow, Rose was the licensee.

The site of the pub is located by a label on a telegraph pole on the opposite side of the road.

William Hobbs lived at Second Drove and described himself as an agricultural labourer and Weslyan local preacher in 1871 and in the late 1800s, a Weslyan Chapel has been built. It closed in June 1985.

Methodist (Weslyan) Chapel. *Photo Courtesy Cambridgeshire Collection*

This is another location recorded by a label on a telegraph pole.

Fond memories of Westmoor chapel. Mr Charlie Murfitt was our Sunday school teacher. My daughter Jennifer was christened on the last ever service to take place, by sister Joyce Rawkins.

St. Owen's School and Church

Photo Courtesy Cambridgeshire collection

The Mission Church of St Owen was built in 1895 in Third Drove, Little Downham, and was dedicated by the then Bishop of Ely, Dr Alwyn Compton, on May 27th 1895. St Owen was Steward of St Etheldreda, Queen and Abbess, who founded the

Its flimsiness caused some concern for the man behind the school being put up. Little Downham vicar, Canon Thornton, became anxious one night when a gale blew up and he climbed to the top of the village church to reassure himself that his school was safe.

Pencils soon made holes in the walls. We carried corks to plug the holes when they caused a draught.

monastery at Ely in 673. The building was built on stilts and made out of paperboard to save on cost and it was also used as a school. The benches had backs which could be swung so that the seats could face either way depending on whether it was the church or the school in use. The first baptisms in the church took place on 30th June 1895 and were Lily and Amelia Harrison of Third Drove, Herbert and Sarah Ann Jordan of Third Drove and Eliza Ann Hobbs of Second Drove. The first child in the School register was Sidney Missin.

The retirement of long-serving teacher, Kate Cooke, was reported:

The pending retirement of Miss Kate Cooke from St. Owen's Church of England School, Third Drove, Little Downham, marks the completion of a strenuous and very remarkable record in the teaching profession.

Starting her career in the days of her girlhood, Miss Cooke has taught in the school, situate in a remote part of Downham parish, for 56 years, without a break, truly a great record of which any teacher might be justly proud.

Residing in the village two miles from the school, Miss Cooke for many years had to cover the distance on foot. The journey included nearly a mile of soft road, often ankle-deep in mud during winter months. Metalling the road later brought the cycle into service, and latterly the advent of the school bus proved a great boon.

During her journeys to and from the school it is estimated that Miss Cooke has covered approximately 49,000 miles, and throughout the whole of her record she has been absent through illness on only one day. She possesses the distinction of having served under five parish rectors, all chairmen of the school managers.

Throughout the greater part of her life Miss Cooke has been associated with work at the parish

> *There were 99 of us in the room one term. The teacher always wanted to reach 100 but we never did. I doubt if we could have squeezed another one in.*

church, and outside school hours she has rendered invaluable services to various village organisations, including the Girl's Club, St. John's Ambulance Brigade and the Women's Institute since its formation nearly 34 years ago. Affectionately known as "Teacher Kate" Miss Cooke was loved by every child she taught. The whole parish of Downham extends heartiest congratulations and wishes for many more years of good health and happiness.

> *I remember the huge tortoise stoves that glass bottles of cows milk were placed around the bottom of to warm up. The toilets were outside at the back of the school.*

At this time Grace Thompson was the head and taught the older pupils. Kate Cooke taught the infants.

A decision was made to close the school in 1962 because of the dwindling number of children attending. It was decided that, as the school was being closed, it was not necessary to provide the building with electricity. In 1968 it was decided to sell the building.

Today the Droves are still largely an agricultural area but with a wider mix of residents.

Downham Lodge is located on Second Drove. Prior to it becoming Downham Lodge it was a home for the elderly. The Chartwell Group purchased the property in 1994 and it was opened as a private residential special needs school for males with emotional and behaviour issues in March 1995. Initially, the school was part of the main building. In 1996 the classroom, workshop and IT suite were built on the site of the old garages. The school and home were jointly registered and inspected by Ofsted. The main house then became the residential side of the site. Over time links were built with the local community which worked really well. Local firms offered work placements for the boys; Ely Tyres, Ely Motorcycles and the local nursery in Little Downham. All of the boys and some staff climbed Snowdon one year and raised over £2000 for the local nursery, supported by Barclays Bank (one of the really big cheques) which the boys handed over.

The school helped somewhere in the region of 40 boys, several of whom still live locally and it was rated as one of the top special needs residential schools at the time.

The school closed in 2012 and Downham Lodge is now a private home.

Ely Eventing Centre is next to Fodder Fen Farm and was started in 1990. It holds equestrian events and has hosted well-known competitors, including royalty.

Dardanelles Cottages in Second Drove are marked by a plaque and are dated 1915. Whether this name commemorates the Dardanelles military campaign is unknown. In 1940 Rose Sugar of Dardanelles Cottages was awarded £200 compensation against London, Midland and Scottish Railways after she fell into a hole on Benfleet station injuring her foot.

The Hexagon House, Second Drove, was a project undertaken by carpenter Kelly Neville in 2005. The house is oak framed with straw bale walls, cedar shingles on the roof and clay plaster on the walls. A ground source heat pump provides underfloor heating and willow grown on-site is used in a furnace. The house uses rainwater harvesting and waste is treated by a reed bed.

Both houses and telegraph poles have trouble staying upright in the soft fen soil.

The project was featured on Channel 4 television programme Grand Designs. Kelly moved to Canada with the idea of pursuing a similar project there. The current owners are extending the house in a similar style.

There is a drove leading from Dunkirk to Pymoor sidings and is marked on modern maps as O Furlong Drove, This seems to be a contraction of the original name of Hoe Furlong.

OCTOBER 12, 1917.

SEVENTH DROVE FARM, DOWNHAM.

On instructions from the executors of the late Mr. Joseph Harrison, Mr. Geo. Comins sold by auction last week the live and dead stock on the Seventh Drove farm, Fodder Fen, Downham, including several Shire mares. The horses and the prices they fetched were: Cheerly, 12 yrs. old, dark chestnut mare, 57gs.; Smiler, 13 yrs. old, chestnut mare, s. Elwyn Tom, 58gs.; Flower, 10 yrs. old, red roan mare, s. Elwyn Tom, 95gs.; Violet, 9 yrs. old, dark chestnut mare, s. Denford Model, 80gs.; Jewell, 3 years old, blue roan mare, 102gs.; Lightsome, 3 yrs. old, bay mare, 75gs.; Gipsy, 3 yrs. old, black mare, 108gs.; Tommy, 3 yrs. old, chestnut gelding, 54gs.; Beauty, 5 yrs. old, bay mare, 85gs. Four Shire colts made 52gs., 48gs., 54gs., and 35gs. respectively, and a red roan filly foal 45gs. A red and white cow, due to calve in October, went for £41 10s., and a red roan shorthorn cow down calving £40, a red and white bull, 2 yrs. old, fetched £14 10s., and heifers made up to £13 10s. A quantity of poultry came under the hammer, fowls making up to 3s. 7d. each. The implements sold included the following: Patent "Nonpariel" 10-coulter corn and seed drill, £39; Progress reaping machine with six sails, £9; two-horse iron crease swing roll with scrapers, £14 10s.; and a three-horse cultivator, £6 10s. An 8 h.p. portable engine, an 8 h.p. double dresser drum, and a straw elevator were sold in one lot for £105; while a manure cart changed hands for £28, and another one for £20.

Dunkirk

The Place Names of Cambridgeshire and the Isle of Ely by P. H. Reany has this to say: "Remote fields are named from distant countries and places such as America, Bunkers Hill, China Close, Dunkirk, Flanders Ground, Gibraltar Close, Isle of Elba, Jamaica, Jerusalem, New England, New Zealand, Scotland and Yorkshire." Therefore this would seem to be a specific example of this tradition.

There was a windmill at the Dunkirk end of Frith Head Drove marked on the 1810 map as Grant's Mill and on later Ordnance Survey maps there is a corn mill to the rear of the buildings on Dunkirk corner.

The Designer Logo Matting Co. Ltd. Currently operates out of a small unit on Dunkirk corner. The company is owned by Vince Burzio and makes doormats with custom-designed logos and exports to Europe, the Middle East and United States.

There is also Wigeon House which was built by a scientist from the British Antarctic Survey to house a collection of ducks and waterfowl.

Hundred Foot Bank

The New Bedford River forms the border of the parish and is also known as the Hundred Foot River because of the distance between the tops of the banks on either side. The banks were controlled by the Bedford Level Corporation and villagers had to apply to the Corporation for permission to build on the bank. The Bedford Level Corporation was wound up in 1920 and its powers passed to the Ouse Drainage Board which in turn became the River Great Ouse Catchment Board. On census returns the Hundred Foot Bank covers an area from Pymoor to the parish and county boundary at the A1101 Littleport to Welney Road.

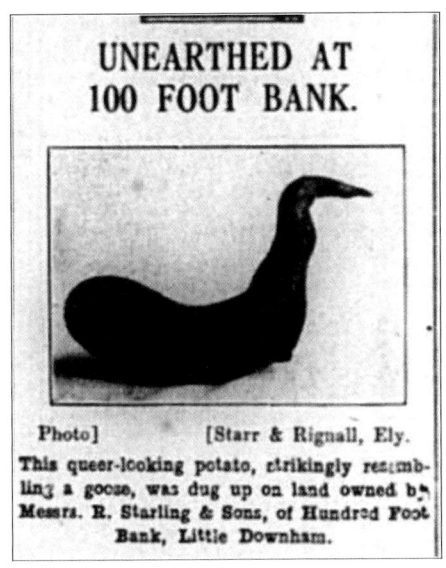

In 1841 there were about 90 entries in the census for families living at the Hundred Foot Bank, mainly agricultural workers but also four publicans, John Foreman, Mendham Martin, Thomas Dewey and James Atkin. John Foreman and Mendham Martin where the landlords of the two pubs in Oxlode, the Crown and the Three Horseshoes but are listed as being on the Hundred Foot Bank. The Five Alls by the pumping station may account for a third entry and there appears to have been a pub across the river on the Wash bank run by the Atkin family of which the name is not recorded.

The later figures are somewhat distorted by parts of Oxlode being recorded in their own right as distinct from the Hundred Foot Bank. The population slowly decreased and by 1861 there were only 29 families and a Methodist chapel has appeared. Another ten years passed and there were two beer houses, the Five Alls with William Stevens as a blacksmith and publican and an unnamed beerhouse on the wash bank run by James Atkin who was a shepherd and publican. The wash bank was the bank on the other side of the river. The Crown and Three Horseshoes were now recorded as being in Oxlode. When James Atkin died his property was taken on by his son John but there is no further mention of a beer house.

The Fives Alls was a popular pub name in the 1800s representing five characters, usually a king, a bishop, a lawyer, a soldier and a countryman, each with a motto underneath. This supposedly represents all levels of society and signifies that the inn is open to all.

The Five Alls had a succession of landlords and owners. It was up for sale in 1860 by W & R Vipan, brewers of Mepal and was described as an old licensed house with a blacksmith's shop attached. Twelve years later it was to let along with an adjoining blacksmith's shop and three cottages. It was then owned by the William Cutlack Brewery of Littleport. Some of the landlords recorded were William Miller, William Johnson, Philip Mann, Robert Moore and John Leaford. In 1904 It was owned by Margaret Gill of St. Mary's Street, Ely.

Methodist Chapel

Next to the pub was the Primitive Methodist Chapel, built in 1878 and now completely dismantled. The final service was conducted by the Rev. Jack Burton of Littleport on 31st October 1965. The closure was brought about by the rapidly diminishing population in this part of the parish.

Primitive Methodist chapel
Photo Courtesy Donald Monk

We lived along the 100ft Bank at Oxlode. We had no mains water laid onto the house so we had to help at night to fill a bath of water from the river, let it settle overnight, and use it the next day. Mother had to boil the water and sometimes there would be a good half-inch of silt in the bottom of the bath.

Memorial Hall

On the corner of New Road and the Hundred Foot Bank stands a derelict building, once Oxlode Memorial Hall. There are commemorative stones in the front wall but these are no longer legible. It was built as a war memorial and opened in 1920.

In 1954 the hall was up for sale by auction, described as of 9 inch brick construction with corrugated iron span roof. There is also a timber built hut and closet.

Oxlode Memorial Hall

OXLODE MEMORIAL HALL.

Successful Sports and Gala to Raise Funds.

THE OPENING CEREMONY.

By the erection of a Memorial Hall for social intercourse at Oxlode, a worthy and permanent war memorial has been established, and has already proved a great boon to the inhabitants of this remote little hamlet in the heart of the Fens. The hall, which was formally opened on Whit-Monday evening, in the presence of a large and representative assembly, is situated at the west end of Willow Farm, near the Hundred-Foot Bank. It is a finely constructed building of brick, with plenty of accommodation, the measurements being 70 feet, by 50 feet. Well ventilated, and with two entrances at the south and west ends, the building has been handsomely furnished for recreational purposes, billiards and other games being provided. Ample heating is provided by a large fireplace at the north end.

The Rev. P. E. Hawkeley presided at the opening ceremony, and was supported by the Rev. H. K. Stallard, Rector of Little Downham, and the Rev. J. E. Roberts, of the Ely Wesley an Church.

The Rev. Hawkeley gave a brief resumé as to the origin of the hall. Mr. Jabez Martin generously gave the land as a site for the hall, and also a donation for £10. Following that the nucleus of a committee was established, and later the following founders were appointed: Messrs. J. C. Wilkin, R. Starling, T. W. O. Mott, H. Stevens, J. H. Pearson, and Mr. and Mrs. Jabez Martin, all of whom gave handsome subscriptions. To augment the fund a successful gala was held on Whit-Monday, 1919, the proceeds amounting to £148, and the hall scheme was continued. About £300 was still required to pay the outstanding debt and equip the hall.

The Rev. Roberts gave an interesting address, in the course of which he dwelt upon the great need for the social life of the country being fostered and improved. He referred to the spirit in which the men went out to the front and the ideals for which they died, and said he was very pleased Oxlode had built that hall.

The Rev. Stallard, who during the war was a Chaplain in the Royal Navy and was stationed at the Crystal Palace, then formally opened the hall. In the course of his address the rev. gentleman enumerated the schemes carried out at the Palace for the social welfare of the men, and emphasised the Rev. Roberts' contention that there was a great need for such clubs and quiet recreation, which led to an improvement in the social life of the community.

A framed scroll bearing the inscription "This hall was erected in memory of the fallen of the parishes of Pymoor and Oxlode," was then hung by the fireplace. Afterwards the Rev. Stallard read out the deed of transfer from Mr. Jabez Martin to the Trustees, and the conditions under which the hall was to be run, and this was signed by each of the founders. A collection in aid of the funds realised £20.

SPORTS AND GALA.

With the object of liquidating the outstanding debt incurred by the erection of the hall a highly successful gala was held in Mr. Watkins' field at Oxlode on Whit-Tuesday afternoon, a large number of visitors being present from all parts. An extensive programme of sports was carried through, and there were generous side shows, including classical half-hour concerts, tennis, shooting gallery, cocoanut shies, etc. Tea was served in a large marquee, and the arrangements reflected considerable credit upon the large Committee responsible.

September 1954: At Wednesday's meeting of the Isle of Ely Highways and Bridges Committee the County Surveyor (Mr A. Morwood) stated that Oxlode Memorial Hall on the Pymoor – Welney road was in a dilapidated condition and was the subject of a planning application for conversion into a dwelling house. That application was refused and, as the building tended to obstruct visibility at a right-angled bend in this road, the committee decided in April to consider the purchase of the building. The surveyor explained that he had asked the agents for the trustees what price was required, but he had now been advised that it had been decided to sell by auction on site. It was agreed to take no action at the present time.

Pumping Station

The biggest building on the Hundred Foot Bank is the pumping station. This has given its name to the area and on some maps, Steam Engine is named as a distinct place.

The pumping station represents the importance of the continuing drainage of the Fens when the Bedford Level was dug in the 17th century. As the land level decreased there was a need to pump the water from the drainage network up into the river and the types of pump are recorded on the side of the pumping station. The current building replaced a windmill in 1830 and has required increasingly powerful pumps. The chimney was removed in the second war to prevent German bombers using it for navigation.

In 1883 the need for a new engineer was reported:

The Littleport and Downham District Commissioners, at their General Half-yearly Meeting, to be held at the Lamb Inn, in Ely, on Wednesday, the 31st day of October next, at 12 o'clock at noon, will be prepared to appoint a person to undertake the working of their large Steam Scoop Wheel Drainage Engine, standing on the bank of the Hundred Foot River, in the parish of Little Downham, near Ely. He must well understand the construction and working of steam drainage engines, and must be competent and prepared to execute all ordinary engine working fittings and repairs. When he is not employed in working the engine or doing engine repairs, he will be required to occupy himself in executing repairs to the bridges of the district, and to hold himself at all times at the service of the Commissioners. The salary will be at the rate of £63 per annum, with house to live in and house coal. Three months notice of putting an end to the service will be required. Each candidate must send his application for the office in his own handwriting, stating his age (accompanied by such testimonials as he may think fit) to me the undersigned on or before Tuesday, the 16th October next. A committee will then make a selection from the candidates for the consideration of the General Meeting of the Commissioners, and the selected candidates only will receive notice to attend the Commissioners meeting, at Ely, on the 31st October next. The person appointed will be required to enter upon his duties not later than the 19th November next, but the Commissioners do not pledge themselves to appoint any of the candidates.

The engine driver recorded in the 1891 census was George Theobold of Welney so it is likely that he was the successful candidate here.

A large company assembled at the Hundred Feet River, Little Downham, on Friday, for the opening of the new pumping plant by the Chairman of the Littleport and Downham Commissioners (Mr Horace J. Martin J. P.) who is inset in the picture, which shows the massive oil engine.

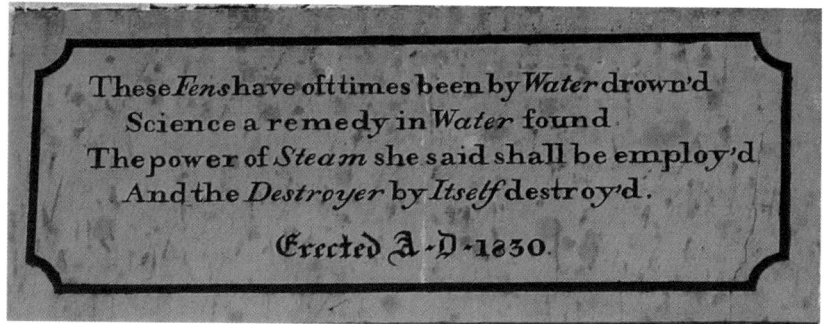

These *Fens* have oft times been by *Water* drown'd
Science a remedy in *Water* found.
The power of *Steam* she said shall be employ'd
And the *Destroyer* by *Itself* destroy'd.

Erected A·D·1830.

Toll House

The road that runs along the Hundred Foot Bank joins the A1101 (Bate's Drove) Littleport to Welney road, on the parish and county boundary. On this corner stands the Toll House. The road between Littleport and the ferry crossing to Welney was turnpiked under an Act of 1824 and the Office of Roads drew up proposals for making a toll road as follows:

An estimate of the expense of making a turnpike road leading from the present turnpike road at or near the town of Littleport in the Isle of Ely towards and unto the present ferry or floating bridge over the hundred feet river in the Parish of Welney in the county of Norfolk
Length of new road 4 miles 2 furlongs Forming road, Materials, Drains, Land, Posts, Rails and Fence   £1426 0s 0d
Contingencies 5 percent   £71 6s 0d
Total   £1497 6s 0d
The expense of making and improving the above road is intended to be defrayed by subscription and may be completed within two years.

In September 1825 the Rev. William Gale Townley, the rector of the parish of Upwell (of which Welney was then a part) leased a strip of land from the Bedford Level Corporation for 99 years in order to build a bridge. The Rev. Townley financed the cost, around £3,000, but was allowed to charge tolls at rates set out in the lease. The bridge was designed by Captain Sir Samuel Brown RN, a naval officer and engineer, and was of a relatively new style, a chain suspension bridge, completed in 1826. The area has been known as 'Suspension Bridge' ever since. In the same year, the North-West District Turnpike Trustees advertised for a loan with which to build the road. The bridge was built with its own toll house, and next to this was the Crown Inn. There are tales of the toll collectors spending much of their time in the pub, having paid a young boy to keep watch outside. It would appear that initially the tolls to cross the bridge were collected in the adjacent toll house for Rev Townley but that the Bedford Level Corporation collected the tolls for the road at the Crown Inn.

In 1828 a meeting was held at the Crown Inn to discuss the installation of toll gates at the end of Bate's Drove and two years later the Bedford Level Corporation wrote to the Rev Townley informing him that they had built a new toll house for the road and leased out the right to collect the tolls.

1 July 1830
Bedford Level Corporation to Rev W. G. Townley.
On the of Lease of Toll House and Tolls at Bate's
Drove in Welney in the Isle of Ely for 17 years
from Lady Day 1830.

Reciting that certain tolls were taken at or near
a public house called the Crown in the Parish of Welney.
Reciting that for public convenience toll has been
removed to the north end of Bate's Drove.
Reciting that such removal took place at
the request of trustees of NW district partly
at their expense and partly of Bedford Level Corporation
Caused erection of a new toll house at this the last
mentioned place which is the property of Bedford Level Corporation
Here witness that the Bedford Level Corporation have leased
all that newly erected Toll House at the north
end of Bate's Drove and the tolls arising therewith
as have here upon been collected by the Bedford Level Corporation.
In trust for the trustees of the road
Annual rent of £5
Trustees to keep same in repair.

The tolls were subsequently let on an annual basis. The rise of railway transport largely halted the improving schemes of turnpike trusts. The system was never properly reformed but from the 1870s Parliament stopped renewing the acts and roads began to revert to local authorities, the last trust vanishing in 1895.

The current owner of the Toll house has her own story to tell:

We moved to the Toll Corner House in March 2017 and the fascination of its history intrigued me. The original build dates back to 1860 with two newer extensions on either side; with years of neglect we wanted a project to eventually restore her beauty again.

Whilst decorating upstairs a few strange occurrences happened; doors would shut, knocking and an electric sander started despite it not being plugged in! In May I restarted my business - Just 4U Cakes, it meant a lot of late nights and this is when I saw our friendly spirit appear. I believe he's the Toll Master. He stands by the laundry door in the original section of the house. This may be something you don't believe in but we've had too many occurrences which we can't place our finger on to think it's anything different. When we moved a lot of people would mention the unfortunate accidents that have been bestowed upon it but despite this we love it here. The sunrises and sunsets are truly beautiful, alongside the friendly villagers who have welcomed us. Getting used to seasons and encountering a few storms have been quite scary at times but we've overcome a lot of challenges and set to stay here. I'm always keen to listen to stories about the Toll House. With uneven floors, rattling slates and a mountain of jobs to be completed; this is home - at last.

Wildfowling

Will Kent was born in Welney and lived in the 1940s in a cottage between the Memorial Hall and the railway bridge at the Hundred Foot Bank in Little Downham. When he died in 1960 Will was described as one of the last remaining wild-fowlers in the country and his life was described in the following article:

```
...Not only one of the last men in England to
shoot in fresh water with a punt gun as part of
his livelihood he was also almost the last man to
make by hand the great grigs and the shorter hives
in which eels are trapped in just the same fashion
as the Saxons trapped them a thousand years or
more ago.
About 1912 or 1913 he, together with two
companions, caught a sturgeon about 9ft long,
```

about 5ft round and which weighed 32 stone. They had to shoot it before it could be got out of the water and were paid £10 for it by a fishmonger.

On dark evenings Will used to sit in his home making his own nets and constructing and sharpening all the tools which he used not only for net making but for peeling willow wands which he grew and seasoned himself.

One bitter day on the washes at Mepal Will killed 160 widgeon with six shots, such shots, rare at any time, are almost unknown today. Many a time on cold winter mornings, with frost glazing the water, he sat in his punt waiting for the first flight of ducks and gaggles of geese, waiting to snatch the rope on the trigger of his 12ft punt gun which would explode into death for many unsuspecting victims.

For several years he was a shepherd on the Hundred Foot Washes watching over ewes and their offspring but patiently waiting for the first frosts…..

Will Kent's uncle, also called Will, lived on the washes opposite Four Balls Farm and his wife would have to row across the river to get milk, newspapers and supplies.

Ice Skating

Ice skating was a popular winter sport in the fens with it reaching a peak in popularity in the 19th century. Welney Washes by the Hundred Foot Bank was a local venue for this sport and Albert Dewsberry was a noted skater. Albert lived at Oxlode for forty years and was rumoured to be the only man to beat the famous fen skater Fish Smart. Albert's career was hindered in 1882 when his left leg was amputated although he continued to compete with an artificial leg still with some success. He was also regarded as a fine player of the concertina.

However, Ice Skating was not the only sport that could take place on the frozen washes as reported in February 1895:

An amusing cricket match has been played on the Welney Wash between teams belonging to Manea and Little Downham. The players, who were on skates, wore old top hats, their wickets were the usual distance apart, fixed on wood, and their bats were shaved down to three inches wide. Manea won by 28 runs, the scores being Manea 98 and Little Downham 70. This novel match created great interest and was watched by many spectators.

Photo Courtesy Cyril Heaps

West Fen and the Holts

West Fen is an area of fenland to the south-west of the parish and includes the Holts, a name now preserved as part of the local nature reserve. The census returns show the inhabitants to be almost entirely farmers and agricultural workers, the notable exception being the pub.

In 1861 Thomas Lister was a publican and ten years later it was John Scarr, farmer and publican. John was followed by Thomas Setchell.

The pub was named as the Oak and also the Royal Oak. In 1904 the landlord was Richard Cornwell and it was owned by A & B Hall of Ely. Apart from the census and licensing returns the Oak makes no appearance in the records. This is a pub that really was in the middle of nowhere. If you take a walk along West Fen Drove, around the corner by the Feoffees Spinney and past the barn onto Short Drove and again round the corner to where the road ends at the nissan hut style metal shed you will be standing by the site of the Oak.

Westmoor Common

Westmoor Common before it was ploughed up
Photo Courtesy Cambridgeshire Collection

Westmoor Common is a triangle of land extending north-west from Guildacre to Adventurers Drove. This was the last remnant of unenclosed common land in the parish. The land was ploughed and farmed in the second war and was not returned to common land.

West Moor Field appears on the edge of 1884 enclosure map as a strip of land between Landfloods Drove and High Road. The landowners were Bishop of Ely, Downham Feoffees, Charles Finch and John Simpson and Wife.

Guildacre Farm stands at the southern end of Westmoor Common. 'The Place Names of Cambridgeshire and The Isle of Ely' states that the name may derive from lands held by the Guild of St. Mary de la Porch and St. Leonard founded in 1475. There have been many recorded residents of this farm throughout history. It was advertised for sale in 1858 as follows:

```
All that very convenient and substantially built
farm homestead, near Westmoor Bridge, and
adjoining the Guild Acre Road, consisting of a
brick-built and thatched cottage, with dairy,
brick-built and tiled barn, stable for six horses,
chaff house, hen house, coal place, a bullock
lodge with steaming room, drill house, cow lodge,
piggeries, calf place, cart lodge and open lodge
for cattle, with two yards and garden, enclosed by
brick walls, and an excellent home close of
pasture, containing 4 acres, 2 roods 14 rods.
Copyhold of the Manor of Downham, tithe rent-
charge £1 13s 4d.
```

Opposite Guildacre Farm is the east end of Landfloods Drove and Bridge Farm. This is where the road crossed the Grunty Fen Drain but this waterway is no longer visible on the landscape and there is no longer a bridge.

On the early census returns this area is referred to as Abisha's Bridge with farmers and agricultural workers living here. In later returns, the name Cop-Hall appears and at Westmoor Common the farming population increases. The name Cophall possibly derives from a copped hall meaning a peaked hall. In 1887 five cottages with gardens and five acres of land were advertised for sale at Copthall.

These were on the site now occupied by a bungalow and farm building.

The name Abisha first appears in the parish registers in 1675 with the baptism of Abisha son of Peter and Frances Watson. The parish accounts of 1699 name Abisha Watson as overseer for the poor so they must have been a family of some account and in 1695 he was renting land at Head Fen from the Feoffees. The name is carried on in the Watson family for a few generations and then falls out of use. There are no other families in Little Downham using the name so this is the likely origin of Abisha's Bridge. By 1911 the name has been abbreviated to Bicer's Bridge and it was still recorded by that name in the 1939 register. This name has now disappeared from the local memory.

The major development here in recent years is Corkers Crisps at Willow Farm. The company was started in 2010 by Ross Taylor to use potatoes grown on the farm. The company has been successful but all the buildings at the site were destroyed by a fire in the summer of 2020. The business is currently being rebuilt.

PARISH PUBS

At the time of writing two pubs are operating in the parish:

The Plough Main Street, Little Downham
The Anchor Main Street, Little Downham

The Following pubs are listed as operating in the parish in the Ely Petty Sessional Division records of 1904:

Crown	Main Street, Little Downham
Red, White and Blue	Main Street, Little Downham
Windmill	Main Street, Little Downham
Club	Main Street, Little Downham
Fox and Hounds	Main Street, Little Downham
Railway Tavern	Main Street, Little Downham
Live and Let Live	Main Street, Little Downham
Spade and Beckett (formerly the Globe)	Little Street, Little Downham
White Horse	White Horse Lane, Little Downham
George and Dragon	Townsend
Brickmaker's Arms	California
Railway Tavern	Black Bank
Oak	West Fen
Dog and Gun	Second Drove
Knife and Steel	Pymoor Corner
Five Alls	Pymoor
Three Horseshoes	Oxlode
Crown	Oxlode

The following pubs were also once operating in the parish but had ceased trading before the 1904 licensing returns.

Wheatsheaf: This was in Main Street, Pymoor (see the Pymoor section).

Red Lion: I can find no definitive record of the location for this pub. However, it was advertised for sale in 1834 with a convenient yard and outbuildings and also a post corn windmill, working two pairs of stones, with half an acre of land. It was occupied by William Casburn but enquiries were to be made to Joseph Little of Oxlode. On the 1841 census, William Casburn is a beer retailer living on Main Street at the end of Chapel Lane and so this is probably the site of the Red Lion.

At the time of writing there are two microbreweries in the parish:

Three Blind Mice Brewery   Black Bank Road

Downham Isle Brewery   Matthew Wren Close (This is about to move to Littleport).

There was also the Fenland Brewery that operated from Cowbridge Hall Road between 1997 and 2008.

Notes